I0790288

ONE CITIZEN ONE VOTE

The Future of Democracy
In America

By

AC Patterson

ISBN: 9798386837488

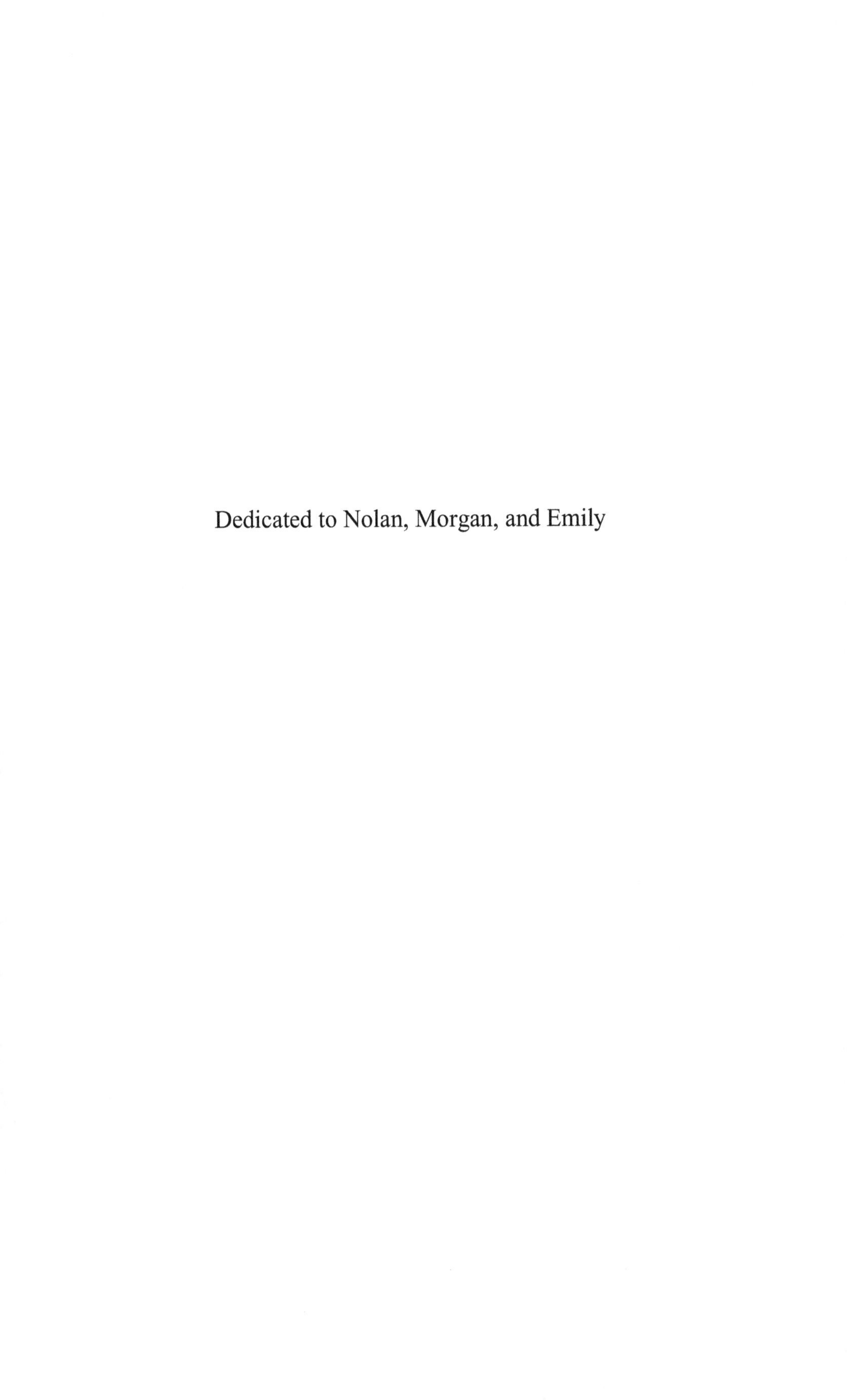

Dedicated to Nolan, Morgan, and Emily

A NOTE TO READERS

Thank you for picking up my book. I'll start by clarifying that this is a work of nonfiction based on my research and experiences. However, please remember that my writing is just one perspective. I've done my best to present information fairly and accurately.

While I've tried to be as thorough as possible in my research, it's always possible that I've made some mistakes or left out important information. I also want to note that my opinions and interpretations are my own, and they may not align with those of others.

I am nonpartisan. I don't belong to or participate in any political Party at the time of this book's publication. I don't work for, consult, own shares in, or receive funding from any company or organization that would benefit from this work. I have disclosed no relevant affiliations beyond their academic appointment.

I hope this book provides a valuable and thought-provoking resource for you, but please don't rely on it as your sole source of information. I encourage you to do your research and form your conclusions.

Sincerely,
AC Patterson

FOREWORD

Nothing sparks controversy in the United States like a discussion about voting, especially around the time of national elections. When speaking of "voting rights," it's interesting how many Americans are confused by the distinction between a right and a privilege.

In this book, I don't advocate partisanship, define voting as an act of patriotism, or encourage mandating the activity of casting a vote. Instead, this book is a history of the U.S. government's practice of granting a political franchise as a right to some U.S. citizens while denying it to others. I also explore alternatives to our current version of democracy.

Arguably, the right to vote in the United States is not a right. Instead, voting is a privilege reserved for a qualified group of birthright and naturalized citizens, but only in certain circumstances. I believe the U.S. government sanctions civic discrimination when it grants the franchise to vote to some citizens while excluding others from the same privilege.

I wrote this to advocate voting rights for all U.S. citizens, including children and those currently denied their equal privilege of citizenship. In doing so, perhaps you'll share this dialog with those around you. If you're a U.S. citizen, this exploration of genuine universal suffrage for all U.S. citizens might resonate in your life.

Table of Contents

Chapter 1 1

Vote for Tomorrow 1

   Civics Education in the U.S 3

   Voting Right or Voting Privilege 7

   Amendments, Slavery and Indentured Servitude 8

   Democracy and Republic 19

   Qualified Privilege 27

   Importance of the Right 34

   Suffrage Through Amendments 35

Chapter 2 .... **39**

   Owning the Franchise 39

   Articles of Confederation into Constitution 40

   Establishing Branches 42

   Courts are Organized 43

   A Bill of Rights 45

   Revolution in Industry 46

   Amendments Expanding 48

   Populists, Women's Rights, and Suffrage 50

   Gender Equality and the ERA 52

   Adopting the Australian Ballot 55

   The Campaign of 1828 57

   15th Amendment and Voter Discrimination 59

   Minority Citizenship and the Vote 62

   1798 Alien and Sedition Acts 64

Chapter 3 .... **67**

   Let's Have a Party 67

   The Democratic-Republican Party is Born 68

   National-Republican Party and Federalism 70

States' Rights Versus Centralized Fed 73

Compromises and Acts of Civil War 74

Social Conservatism and Liberalism..............................78

Political Partisanship 81

Gerrymandering, Voter IDs, Roll Purges 82

Party Organization..87

Conventions, Primaries, and Caucuses..........................88

Chapter 4..**93**

Citizenship, Rights, and Fights......................................93

Citizenship and Immigration..98

Voting Rights Accorded by Status 103

Immigration and Paths to Citizenship 106

Declaring Independence..109

Age Discrimination and Children's Rights 111

Modern Discrimination and Inequality 115

Contemporary Fights for Rights...................................116

Equal Protection 119

Chapter 5..**125**

We Need Money..125

Platforms and Campaigns...127

How About Some Political Action................................128

Look, We're On TV 133

Campaign to the Stars 137

It's All in the Cards 138

It's Mostly a Rally..139

A Web of Dos, Don'ts, and Maybes 141

Chapter 6..**145**

Reform School..**145**

Ranked Choice: Fixing Broken Elections 149

Transparency to End Gerrymandering 150

Inclusive Voting in Primaries 151

Expand Absentee Voting 152

Transform Election Funding 153

Enact Reasonable Term Limits 155

Automatic Voter Registration 156

Lobbying and Lobbyist Bundling 158

The Revolving Door Should Be Closed 161

End Fundraising at Work 162

Contributions in the Sunshine 164

Chapter 7 ....**167**

The Spirit of America 167

The American Dream: Citizenship and Inclusion 168

A Right to Vote: Suffrage in the Present Day 169

Political Participation and the Role of Youth 170

The Struggle for Social Justice 171

Civic Engagement and Responsible Citizenship 172

American Spirit and the Power of Diversity 173

The Protection of Individual Rights 174

American Spirit and the Importance of Education 174

Political Parties and the American Government 175

American Spirit and the Global Community 176

Chapter 8 ....**179**

A New Quest for Suffrage 179

Counting Heads 181

The Dream of True Universal Suffrage 187

Voices of the Future 188

Representative Democracy 195

REFERENCES 199

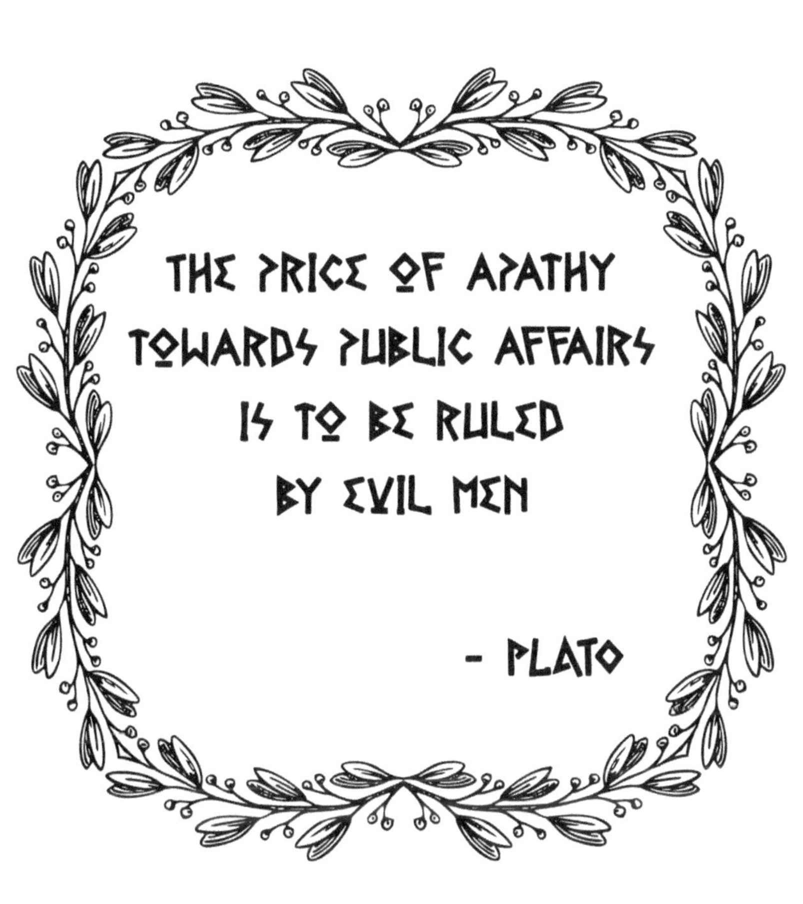
THE PRICE OF APATHY
TOWARDS PUBLIC AFFAIRS
IS TO BE RULED
BY EVIL MEN

- PLATO

Chapter 1

Vote for Tomorrow

Imagine a country where all citizens of the United States have equal and unfettered access to the ballot box. Every citizen has the right to vote, regardless of race, ethnicity, age, religion, gender, sexual orientation, disability, or geographic location. A country where the political process gives every citizen an equal say and every vote has the same weight.

In this country, no discriminatory voting practices or barriers to voting can disproportionately affect certain groups of people. No voter suppression tactics, such as strict voter identification laws, purges of voter rolls, or gerrymandering, undermine the voting rights of certain groups.

Citizens can register to vote easily and efficiently, and polling places are accessible to everyone. People can cast their ballots privately and securely without fear of intimidation or coercion.

In this country, the political process is open and transparent, and every citizen has the opportunity to participate in it. This country would conduct political campaigns fairly and equitably and give every candidate an equal chance to make their case to the voters.

These imaginings seem idealistic but are worth striving for in a democracy. The right to vote is essential to the functioning of a democratic society. Ensuring all citizens have equal and unfettered access to the ballot box is a critical step toward creating a more equitable and just society. The United States could improve the political system by working toward this goal. We could choose a system fully representative of the people's will.

Today, children are the most significant number of our U.S. citizens denied voting rights. According to the United States Census Bureau's 2020 population estimates, there were approximately 73.1 million children in the United States under the age of 18. It should be noted that it's impossible to determine how many of those children are legal U.S. citizens without additional information, such as the immigration status of their parents. Still, based on reasonable estimates, it's fair to presume that at least 90 percent or 65.9 million are.

There are other democratic countries in the world where their citizens' children can vote in their elections, either partially or fully. One example is Austria, where 16- and 17-year-olds vote in national and local elections. This policy was implemented in 2007 and has successfully increased youth participation in their political process.

Another country that allows older children to vote is Scotland, where 16- and 17-year-olds can vote in local and parliamentary elections. This policy was introduced in 2015 and successfully increased youth participation there. A few smaller countries also allow children to vote, such as Brazil and the Isle of Man, where children as young as 16 can vote in local elections.

Many candid discussions have been about allowing citizen children to vote in the United States. Still, there are a few challenges to implementing this as a national policy. One common concern is that children may not have the same life experience and knowledge level as adults, which could affect their ability to make informed decisions at the ballot box. Additionally, there are concerns about the potential for manipulation or coercion of young voters by adults.

It is possible for the U.S. to implement child voting equitably, but is that practical, and who would benefit politically? The latter question has become central to the opposition's argument, and it's obvious it emanates from a fear of unknown outcomes contrary to the interests of one political party or another. These are topics explored later in this book.

Meanwhile, one option could be to gradually extend the right to vote to younger and younger age groups, starting with 16- and 17-year-olds, slowly lowering the voting age as children gain more life experience and maturity in society. The maturity level of 16- and 17-year-olds is not the same today as when the U.S. passed the 26th Amendment in 1971, lowering the voting age for all citizens to 18. A slow method of adoption would allow for a gradual transition, allowing children to learn about the political process before fully participating.

The U.S. could implement mandatory civic education for children, similar to civic education mandates of other countries, as another option. This system would ensure that young people understand the political process and the issues at stake before they're allowed to vote.

Civics Education in the U.S.

The founders of the United States believed education should be widely available to all citizens to develop their skills in critical thinking, debate, and good citizenship. They believed education would enable citizens to actively participate in self-governance and work toward the common good rather than simply being blindly loyal to the State or its leaders. They saw being American as something that required learning and effort.

Currently, U.S. students don't have equal access to comprehensive civics education in our country. In the past, the nation required high school students to take three separate courses in civics and government. However, the availability of these courses has decreased over time as the country's school curriculum has become more focused on other subjects. As a result, many U.S. students may not receive the same level of civics instruction as their past peers.

There's a problem with access to civics education in the United States too. Data from the National Education Association shows that only 25% of students achieve proficiency in the NAEP Civics Assessment (National Center for Education Statistics, 2021). Additionally, students from wealthy, white backgrounds are much more likely to excel in this subject than African-American and Hispanic students from low-income households. Students in more affluent school districts are more likely to receive a better education in civics than those in low-income and predominantly minority schools.

The issue with civics education is not that students don't receive any instruction in this subject. All 50 States require some form of civics or government education, and nearly 90% of all students take at least one civics class. However, the problem is that these classes often rely solely on memorizing facts rather than providing practical, hands-on experiences such as participating in community service, engaging in debates, discussing current events, simulating democratic processes, or actual participation in the democratic process.

Misunderstandings of the issue form the basis of some of the most commonly suggested solutions to the problems with civics education. The National Education Association reports (National Education Association, 2021) that even in States that mandate civics education, best practices are often not followed.

For example, several States have implemented a requirement for students to pass the U.S. citizenship exam before graduating high school. However, heavy emphasis on memorization can reduce students' chances of acquiring more valuable civic skills.

There are several potential solutions to the problems with civics education in the United States. One robust solution is to address barriers that currently exist for civics educators.

A survey conducted by the Center for Information & Research on Civic Learning and Engagement (Center for Information & Research on Civic Learning and Engagement, 2019) found that 25% of teachers believed that parents would object if they taught about politics in a civics or government class. This belief was due to the current political climate in the country. Additionally, only 38% of teachers felt that their school district would support their efforts to teach civics. When teachers perceive that they have support, they're more likely to use effective teaching methods in their civics classes.

Over the past few decades, there's been a decrease in various indicators of civic involvement in the United States, including political engagement. Trust in government and other major social institutions is also low. However, younger adults tend to have a more positive view of the public sector.

Despite an overall increase in education levels, political knowledge has remained unchanged for a long time. Improving civics education might help address some of these negative trends.

We generally reserve the right to vote in the U.S. for citizens 18 or older. However, a few U.S. States allow persons under 18 to participate in local or state elections in certain circumstances. The nation must consider any policy allowing children to vote in the United States. Any such policy implemented would also need to consider this issue's unique challenges and opportunities.

One example is the State of Maryland, which allows 16- and 17-year-olds to pre-register to vote in national elections. When they turn 18, they'll automatically be registered to vote and receive their voter registration card in the mail. Maryland also allows 17-year-olds to vote in primary elections if they'll be 18 by the time of the general election. This policy encourages young people to become engaged in the national political process and to start thinking about their role as U.S. citizens at an earlier age.

Takoma Park, Maryland, allows 16- and 17-year-olds to vote in local elections. This Maryland city implemented its policy in 2013 to encourage young people to get involved in their community and actively participate in local decision-making.

A few other States, such as Oregon and California, have considered proposals to lower the voting age to 17 or 16, but these proposals haven't been successful. Opponents of lowering the voting age argue that young people aren't mature enough to make informed decisions about political issues and that their parents or peers may influence them. "Lowering the voting age supporters" argue that young people, affected by political decisions like adults, should have a say in representation. They also argue that young people should have a say in decisions about their community.

It's also important to note that variations of the opposition's arguments about our younger citizens' maturity or mental capacity in voting aren't far removed from those used to exclude other groups from voting in this country's not-so-recent past. Constitutional Amendments subsequently struck down these substantially equivalent arguments.

While the majority of States in the U.S. don't allow persons under the age of 18 to vote in elections, a small number of States and localities have implemented policies to allow some young people to participate in the political process. These policies often encourage young people to become engaged in their community and consider their role as citizens at an earlier age.

Engaging young people in the political process and fostering a sense of civic responsibility at a young age can have numerous benefits for the individual and society. For young people, engaging in their communities and learning about their role as citizens can provide a sense of purpose and direction. It can also help them develop essential skills such as critical thinking, problem-solving, and communication, which can be helpful in their personal and professional lives. Additionally, being politically active and engaged can help young people feel like they have a voice and make a difference in their community and future.

Engaging our young people in the political process can help create a more informed and active citizenry for a future society. It can also help to promote democracy and ensure we hear the voices of all members of the community. Furthermore, fostering a sense of civic responsibility in young people can help to create a more cohesive and harmonious society, as individuals who feel invested in their community are more likely to work towards the common good.

There are many ways that political policies can encourage young people to become engaged in their community and to think about their role as citizens. These can include initiatives such as voter education and registration drives, community service programs, and leadership development opportunities. We can implement these policies at the local, state, or national level, targeting specific groups of young people, or they could be implemented more broadly.

Voting Right or Voting Privilege

Many Americans are confused by the distinction between a right and a privilege regarding their voting right. This confusion stems from a misunderstanding of the context in which the U.S. defines the word "right." A formal "right" is a fundamental entitlement guaranteed to all individuals by the government or society in which they live. On the other hand, a franchise is a conditional "right or privilege" granted to a specific group of individuals, often based on certain criteria or qualifications. The latter defines the "right" to vote in the United States.

U.S. voting "right" is granted to citizens by the government as a political franchise or privilege. The U.S. Constitution didn't initially include the right to vote for all citizens. Later legislation added or "amended" the voting rights of different groups of citizens to the Constitution throughout the centuries.

In the United States, the right to vote is generally considered a privilege granted to citizens by the government. We refer to the right to vote as a "right" because it's essential for democratic participation and is therefore protected by the Constitution and federal laws. Initially, we didn't grant the right to vote to all citizens in the United States. Only white male property owners were allowed to vote when the Constitution was adopted. The original draft of the Constitution excluded women, people of color, children, and poor white men from participating by voting in the political process.

Over time, we've extended the right to vote to more and more groups of citizens through amendments to the Constitution and other legal changes. For example, the 15th Amendment, adopted in 1870, granted African-American men and men of all economic conditions the right to vote. The 19th Amendment, adopted in 1920, gave women the right to vote. The 26th Amendment, adopted in 1971, lowered the voting age to 18 for all citizens.

Other groups, such as Native Americans and people with disabilities, have also struggled to gain the right to vote and have had to fight for equal access to the polls. Expanding the franchise in the United States has been a long and sometimes complex process. Still, it's also been essential to the country's history and its commitment to democratic values.

One recent and disturbing trend representative of voter suppression tactics is being employed by a small number of partisan elected representatives serving in the U.S. Congress. At the time of this book's publication, bills were being debated to significantly restrict access to the polls for younger and older citizens based on ever stricter identification requirements. This sort of political activity isn't new, as the U.S. has had a long history of denying the vote in our limited form of representative democracy. Fortunately for our citizenry, the Rule of Law eventually prevails, but the struggle for voting rights in the United States continues.

Amendments, Slavery and Indentured Servitude

The 13th Amendment, adopted in 1865, abolished slavery and involuntary servitude, except as a punishment for a crime. The 13th Amendment significantly impacted African-Americans' rights and United States history. This amendment, the first of what are known as "the Reconstruction Amendments," adopted after the Civil War, abolished slavery and involuntary servitude in most cases. This Amendment's intention would have fully served social justice. However, the Amendment's exclusion of the total abolition of indentured servitude for those convicted of a crime has perpetuated many human rights arguments that once existed supporting the abolition of the practice of slavery.

Today, many argue that privatizing the nation's prisons and the exponential growth of the country's imprisoned population have combined to become exploitive of prisoner labor. Combined with the disproportionate representation in prison populations by ethnic and racial minorities among those incarcerated, this indicates concern and a demonstrated need to revisit, perhaps even revise, the wording of the 13th Amendment, entirely abolishing the practice of involuntary servitude in the United States.

The Reconstruction Amendments were a series of additions to the United States Constitution. These amendments, which include the 13th, 14th, and 15th Amendments, were intended to fundamentally change the social and political landscape of the United States by granting new rights and protections to African-Americans and other marginalized groups.

As stated, the 13th Amendment abolished slavery and involuntary servitude in the U.S. The 13th Amendment states: "Neither slavery nor involuntary servitude except as a punishment for crime whereof the party shall have been duly convicted, shall exist within the United States, or any place subject to their jurisdiction." This amendment significantly impacted the rights of African-Americans, as many were in bondage as enslaved people before its adoption. The law marked the beginning of a new era in which the U.S. granted African-Americans freedom and the rights and protections of citizenship, but the privilege to vote was elusory.

The 14th Amendment, adopted in 1868, granted citizenship to "all persons born or naturalized in the United States," which included African-Americans. The 14th Amendment also included the Equal Protection Clause, which prohibits states from denying any person "equal protection of the laws." The courts use this clause to strike down discriminatory laws and practices disproportionately affecting minority groups. It's been an essential tool in the ongoing struggle for civil rights and equality for all U.S. citizens.

The 15th Amendment, adopted in 1870, granted African-American men the right to vote. The text of the 15th Amendment states: "The right of citizens of the United States to vote shall not be denied or abridged by the United States or by any State on account of race, color, or previous condition of servitude." This amendment intended to ensure that African-American men could fully participate in the political process and have a say in the policies and decisions that affected their lives. Sadly, it would be a long time and well into the next century before this became a reality.

The Reconstruction Amendments had a significant impact on the social and political landscape of the United States. These Amendments marked a substantial shift in how we treated African-Americans and other marginalized groups, granting them new rights and protections previously unavailable. For example, the 13th Amendment ended the practice of slavery, which had been a central institution of the territorial colonies of the United States for more than 200 years, with the first record indicating the practice of slavery in the U.S. colonies, at Jamestown plantation in Virginia, in 1619.

The 14th Amendment granted African-Americans the full rights and protections of citizenship, including the right to due process and equal protection under the law. And the 15th Amendment ensured that African-Americans could fully participate in the political process and have a say in the policies and decisions that affected their lives.

The Reconstruction Amendments didn't immediately resolve the problem of racial inequality in the United States, though. Despite adopting these amendments, the U.S. still denied many African-Americans their rights, subjecting them to discrimination and segregation. It wasn't until the passage of the Civil Rights Act of 1964 and the Voting Rights Act of 1965 that African-Americans could fully exercise their rights as citizens, including the right to vote. The Reconstruction Amendments have had a lasting impact on the United States and have played a crucial role in the ongoing struggle for civil rights and equality for all our citizens.

It's interesting to note the text of the 13th Amendment didn't abolish involuntary servitude altogether. As mentioned, it states: "Neither slavery nor involuntary servitude except as a punishment for crime whereof the party shall have been duly convicted, shall exist within the United States, or any place subject to their jurisdiction."

It's important to note that the 13th Amendment is interpreted to have two meanings. The first abolishes slavery and involuntary servitude in all circumstances except for punishment for a crime. This interpretation means it's illegal to hold someone in bondage or to force them to work against their will unless they've been convicted of a crime and are serving a sentence as part of their punishment. The second meaning, or exclusion of convicted criminals from being indentured, continues the practice of indentured servitude in this country today. In another book, the author explores this practice in much greater detail. [See acpatterson.com.]

The courts defined involuntary servitude as work or service exacted from a person under threat of punishment and for which the person has not volunteered. Involuntary servitude can include situations where we force people to work through physical or economic coercion or give them no choice about whether to work.

Examples of involuntary servitude that the courts have struck down as unconstitutional include forced labor camps, debt bondage, and human trafficking. We've deemed these practices a violation of the 13th Amendment's prohibition on involuntary servitude. However, today's for-profit private prison corporations, sanctioned by the U.S., state, and local governments, routinely use prison labor to manufacture commercial products and goods or provide for-profit services. Many ethical and legal concerns about these practices directly related to the 13th Amendment's abolition of slavery and the conditional abolition of involuntary servitude continue to be debated and litigated.

Still, adopting the 13th Amendment significantly impacted the lives of African-Americans held in bondage as enslaved people for centuries. This law marked the beginning of a new era in which the U.S. granted African-Americans freedom, rights, and protections of citizenship. However, it would be a long time before that would become a reality.

Despite adopting the 13th Amendment, we still denied many African-Americans their rights and subjected them to discrimination and segregation. It wasn't until the passage of the Civil Rights Act of 1964 and the Voting Rights Act of 1965 that African-Americans could fully exercise their rights as citizens, including the right to vote.

The 13th Amendment played a crucial role in the history of the United States, though, especially in the struggle for civil rights and equality for all citizens. While it significantly impacted the right to vote for African-Americans, it's important to note that the 13th didn't explicitly grant African-Americans the right to vote.

In the aftermath of the Civil War, the amendment's primary purpose was to abolish slavery and involuntary servitude, except as a punishment for a crime. While the 13th Amendment marked a significant step toward ending the institution of slavery in the United States, it didn't address other issues related to civil rights and equality. At its ratification, the U.S. still denied many African-Americans fundamental rights and freedoms, such as the right to a fair trial and the right to own property.

One reason the 13th Amendment didn't explicitly grant African-Americans the right to vote was that the main focus of the Amendment was to end slavery, not to grant civil rights to the newly freed enslaved. Many lawmakers at the time, just as today, believed voting was a privilege, not a right. Further, they argued African-Americans weren't ready to vote for many of the same reasons other groups have been denied the vote since then. Some lawmakers also argued that African-Americans weren't intelligent or educated enough to participate in the democratic process. These arguments are not dissimilar from those currently used as a basis for denying U.S. citizen children voting rights.

Another reason was many Southern states resisted granting African-Americans this right. Even some Northern states had laws restricting African-Americans' voting right. These states used tactics like literacy tests and poll taxes to prevent African-Americans from voting. It wasn't until the passage of the 14th and 15th Amendments and the Voting Rights Act of 1965 that African-Americans in the United States could exercise the right to vote entirely.

The 14th Amendment, ratified in 1868, granted citizenship to "all persons born or naturalized in the United States," which included African-Americans. It gave citizenship to all persons born or naturalized and intended to protect their civil rights. This Amendment marked a significant change from the previous conditions of citizenship in the United States, which the U.S. had formerly defined primarily by race and ancestry.

Before the 14th Amendment, the country based its citizenship on the principle of "jus soli," or "right of the soil," which granted citizenship to individuals born within the territory of the United States, regardless of their parent's citizenship status. However, this principle wasn't applied consistently, and there were many exceptions and limitations. For example, we didn't grant citizenship to Native Americans until 1924, and we didn't recognize African-Americans as full citizens until after the Civil War.

The 14th Amendment, part of the Reconstruction Amendments, was adopted after the Civil War to reconstruct the United States and grant the newly freed enslaved civil rights. The 14th Amendment aimed to establish African-Americans as full citizens with all the rights and privileges of other citizens.

The 14th Amendment granting citizenship to "all persons born or naturalized in the United States" was purposefully drafted to overturn the Supreme Court's Dred Scott decision. Dred Scott denied citizenship to African-Americans and declared them "beings of an inferior order and altogether unfit to associate with the white race." The Dred Scott decision was a landmark case in United States history that significantly impacted voting rights, particularly for African-Americans.

Dred Scott was an African-American man who sued for his freedom in 1846, arguing that he had become free after living in states where slavery was illegal. The Supreme Court eventually heard the case and ruled against Scott in 1857. This ruling became an indelible stain on our nation's history, much like the institution of slavery. Our nation's highest Court made this decision, which today is viewed as immoral.

In the Dred Scott decision, the Supreme Court held that African-Americans, whether freed or enslaved, weren't citizens of the United States. As such, they weren't entitled to the rights and protections afforded to citizens. The Dred decision declared that

African-Americans were "beings of an inferior order, and altogether unfit to associate with the white race, either in social or political relations and are so far inferior that they had no rights which the white man was bound to respect." The Dred Scott decision profoundly impacted African-Americans in many ways but effectively denied them the right to vote.

Before the Civil War, many states had imposed various restrictions on rights, such as property requirements and literacy tests, that effectively excluded African-Americans from participating in the democratic process. The Dred Scott decision exacerbated these restrictions by denying the legal status of citizens, a necessary prerequisite for voting in many states.

The Dred Scott decision also established the legal principle that African-Americans were inferior to whites and not entitled to the same rights and protections. Dred Scott justified segregation and discrimination. The decision was widely condemned by abolitionists and civil rights advocates, contributing to the growing tensions that eventually led to the Civil War.

The 14th Amendment granted citizenship to all persons born or naturalized in the United States and protected civil rights, including those of African-Americans. This amendment overturned the Dred Scott decision, ushering in a new era.

The 14th Amendment also contained provisions that guaranteed due process and equal protection of the law, intended to prevent states from denying African-Americans civil rights, including the right to vote. However, it took decades of activism and many struggles to secure the full rights and freedoms promised by the 14th Amendment. The Voting Rights Act of 1965 was necessary for many to gain the right to vote.

The 14th Amendment also specified that U.S. citizenship would be determined by birth or naturalization, establishing a means of identifying persons as citizens. Birthright citizenship, or "jus soli," was recognized as the primary means of acquiring citizenship, but the Amendment also recognized naturalization as a means of becoming a citizen. This law allowed individuals who weren't born in the United

States but who met specific requirements to become citizens through a process known as naturalization. It was a radical departure from previous laws and practices, which excluded African-Americans from citizenship based on race.

Naturalization is the process by which a person who is not a citizen of the United States can become a citizen. To be eligible for naturalization, an individual must meet specific requirements, such as being at least 18 years old, being a permanent resident of the United States, and demonstrating good moral character. Naturalization also requires the applicant to pass a test on the history and government of the United States. The amendment recognized naturalization as a means of acquiring citizenship, which allowed individuals who weren't born in the United States to become citizens if they met the requirements.

The 14th Amendment also includes the "Equal Protection Clause," which prohibits states from denying any person "equal protection of U.S. laws." The courts have used this clause to strike down discriminatory voting laws that disproportionately affect minority groups.

The "Equal Protection Clause," contained within the 14th Amendment, prohibits states from enacting laws that discriminate against certain groups of people or that treat people differently based on characteristics such as race, ethnicity, religion, gender, or national origin. The Clause applies to all levels of government, including federal, state, and local, and it applies to all branches of government, including the legislative, executive, and judicial.

The Equal Protection Clause challenges laws and practices that discriminate against certain minority groups of people, including African-Americans. This Clause has significantly impacted voting rights in the United States. Before the adoption of the 14th Amendment, many states had laws that restricted the right to vote based on race, ethnicity, or other factors, such as property requirements and literacy tests.

The Equal Protection Clause has also been used to challenge and overturn many other laws that violated the principle of equal protection. In the landmark case of Harper v. Virginia Board of Elections (1966), the Supreme Court held that Virginia's poll tax violated the Equal Protection Clause. The tax meant the right to vote wasn't applied equally to all voters. The Court declared that "voter qualifications have no relation to wealth" and that the poll tax was unconstitutional. The decision to strike down the poll tax helped remove one of the barriers used to deny the right to vote to many minority groups.

The 14th Amendment's Clause has also challenged laws and practices that discriminate against minority groups in other areas, such as education, employment, housing, and access to public facilities. This Clause has played a central role in the ongoing struggle for civil rights and equality in the United States. It has profoundly impacted voting rights and other civil rights issues.

The Equal Protection Clause has also challenged bias in political redistricting, voter ID laws, and voter suppression in several voting rights cases. For example, in the case of Baker v. Carr (1962), the Supreme Court held that states must redraw their legislative districts. The Court sought to ensure equal representation of the population and protect the right to vote.

In Shelby County v. Holder (2013), the Court struck down a key provision of the Voting Rights Act of 1965, used to challenge discriminatory voting practices in states with a history of racial discrimination. The decision in Shelby County v. Holder was widely criticized as a setback for voting rights, making it more difficult for minority groups to challenge discriminatory voting practices.

The Shelby County v. Holder decision, issued by the United States Supreme Court in 2013, was a significant setback. The case concerned a provision of the Voting Rights Act of 1965 known as the "preclearance" requirement, which mandated that certain states and jurisdictions with a history of racial discrimination in voting had to seek approval from the federal government before making any changes to their voting laws or procedures.

In the Shelby County case, the Court ruled that the preclearance requirement was unconstitutional, as it was based on decades-old data and did not consider the significant progress in addressing racial discrimination in voting. The Court's decision effectively struck down the preclearance requirement, freeing the states and jurisdictions previously covered to change their voting laws without federal approval.

The Shelby County decision significantly impacted voting rights in the United States by removing the critical protection against voter suppression and discrimination. Before the decision, the preclearance requirement blocked numerous voting laws and procedures as subject to federal review.

Civil rights groups and voting rights advocates widely criticize the Shelby County decision, arguing that it weakens protections for minority voters and could increase voter suppression. In the years following the decision, several states implemented voting laws criticized as discriminatory, including strict voter ID laws, purges of voter rolls, and restrictions on early voting. States have been challenged for these laws in various courts, and the ongoing debate over voting rights continues to be controversial and contentious in the United States.

The 15th Amendment, ratified in 1870, expressly prohibited states from denying the right to vote to citizens based on race, color, or previous condition of servitude. The passage of this amendment marked a significant change from earlier conditions, as many states had laws that restricted the right to vote based on these factors, effectively denying the vote to many minority groups, including African-Americans.

One reason the 15th Amendment expressly prohibited states from denying the right to vote to citizens based on race, color, or previous condition of servitude was to address the legacy of slavery and racial discrimination in the United States. As stated, the U.S. adopted the 15th Amendment as part of a series of Reconstruction Amendments to "reconstruct" the country after the war and extend civil rights to the newly freed enslaved. The 15th Amendment ensured African-Americans, previously denied the right to vote for many years, could fully participate in the democratic process. Still, the reality of that right didn't fully exist for them until the mid-1960s.

Before the adoption of the 15th Amendment, many states had laws that restricted the right to vote based on an array of factors such as race, ethnicity, and property ownership. The 15th Amendment intended to ensure that all citizens, regardless of race or ethnicity, receive equal treatment under the law. While the 15th Amendment prohibited states from denying the right to vote to citizens based on race, color, or previous condition of servitude, it didn't enjoy widespread enforcement for a long time. This amendment addressed the laws and practices used to deny the right to vote to minority groups, such as literacy tests, poll taxes, and other voter suppression tactics, but States routinely circumvented it. Adopting the 15th Amendment, at least initially, in spirit, ended laws and practices that discriminated against African-Americans and other minorities, allowing them to participate effectively in the democratic process.

The 13th, 14th, and 15th Amendments to the United States Constitution, adopted in the aftermath of the Civil War, granted citizenship and civil rights to many Americans and prohibited states from denying the right to vote based on race, color, or previous condition of servitude. However, it took decades of determined activism, and many struggles to enforce these Amendments and secure the full rights and freedoms promised to Americans.

Many states continued to use discriminatory practices like literacy tests and poll taxes long after the passage of these Amendments, solely to deny African-Americans the right to vote. Even decades after adopting these Amendments, it wasn't until the Voting Rights Act of 1965 prohibited these practices and provided enforced federal oversight of elections that African-Americans and other similarly marginalized citizens could fully exercise their right to vote.

Expanding the right to more and more groups of citizens has significantly impacted the political landscape of the United States. For example, including women and African-Americans as voters have led to more diverse candidates' election to public office. It's also given these groups a more significant say in the policies and decisions that affect their lives.

Voting rights are an essential aspect of democratic participation. The Constitution and various federal laws protect it. We can and should expand the franchise to vote to include more groups of our nation's legal citizens currently denied the privilege, and we must do more work to enable all U.S. citizens to exercise their right to vote.

Democracy and Republic

The United States is a complex political system combining elements of both a democracy and a republic. Whether the United States is a democracy or a republic is often debated by Americans who are concerned with ensuring that their government serves the needs of the people. It's important to understand that the United States can be accurately described as a democracy and a republic, even though these terms are not mutually exclusive.

The United States is technically a representative democracy, meaning citizens hold ultimate political power by electing representatives to make decisions on their behalf. The U.S. is not a direct democracy, where citizens make decisions directly without intermediaries. Still, it does have elements of direct democracy in some states and localities, such as ballot initiatives and referenda, which allow citizens to enact, change, or repeal laws directly. In a representative democracy, citizens participate in the democratic process by voting in elections to choose their representatives, who then make decisions on their behalf. This system is distinct from the ancient Greek concept of democracy, a direct democracy where eligible citizens congregated to make decisions themselves.

Five scholars wrote about their belief that the American system is a democracy. They were John Adams, Thomas Jefferson, Noah Webster, Justice James Wilson, and Chief Justice John Marshall. The term "democracy" is not used in the U.S. Constitution, though reasons exist for this and the scholars' use of the word.

The Founders of the United States avoided using the term "democracy" in the Constitution because they were wary of pure democracy, in which people make all decisions directly. They believed it could lead to mob rule and the tyranny of the majority. The Founders sought to create a more balanced system of government, one in which the power of the people was checked and balanced by other branches and levels of government. As a result, the Constitution established a federal system of government, separation of powers, and a system of checks and balances rather than a pure democracy.

Many scholars and leaders have used the term. "democracy" to refer to the American system of government. For example, John Adams wrote that the United States was "a government of laws, and not of men" and "a democracy if you can keep it." In this statement, Adams recognized that the American system of government was a democratic one in which the people had a say in the decisions that affected their lives. Still, he also acknowledged that democracy required the active participation and engagement of the people to be successful.

Thomas Jefferson also described the United States as a democracy, writing it as "a government by the people, for the people." Jefferson believed that the American system was a democratic one. He meant "the people" had a direct say in the decisions that affected their lives. He also argued that the United States was "the world's best hope" for democracy and represented a model for other countries to follow.

Noah Webster, Justice James Wilson, and Chief Justice John Marshall were all influential figures in American history. Each of them used the term "democracy" to refer to the American system of government. They, too, believed the government was a democratic one.

For example, Noah Webster was a lexicographer, writer, and political commentator best known for his dictionary, which helped to standardize the English language in the United States. In his writings, Webster described the United States as a democracy. Webster defined democracy as a "government in which the supreme power [rests] in the hands of the people, exercised by themselves or their representatives."

James Wilson was a Founding Father, a signer of the Declaration of Independence, and a member of the Constitutional Convention. He served as an Associate Justice of the Supreme Court from 1789 to 1798. Wilson described the U.S. as a democracy in his writings and argued that the Constitution protected the people's rights and preserved democratic principles.

John Marshall was the Chief Justice of the Supreme Court from 1801 to 1835. He is widely considered one of the most influential figures in American legal history. Marshall often referred to the United States as a democracy in his judicial opinions. He also argued that the Constitution protected the rights of the people and preserved democratic principles. In particular, these men viewed American democracy as a "representative democracy." Since the government was one in which citizens elect representatives to make decisions on their behalf, they described it as a form of democracy. This understanding of "representative democracy" as a "form of democracy" is shared by many people today. The U.S. is also a republic because our elected representatives exercise political power.

The United States is often called a "representative democracy." A representative democracy is one in which elected representatives exercise political power on behalf of the people. In a representative democracy, citizens elect representatives to make decisions and act on their behalf rather than making decisions directly. This form of democracy gives the people a say in the decisions affecting their lives while allowing the government to function efficiently and effectively, hypothetically, in the case of the United States. Hypothetically, this form of government has an element of trust, and our elected representatives have betrayed that trust in the past. This fact and its potential reoccurrence could devastate the democratic ideology upon which this country was founded. This potential is among the most powerful arguments for revisiting our choice of representative democracy versus a true democracy.

Modern-day corruption of our elected political representatives, those who act in their elected capacities contrary to our laws, has become a commonplace concern to our nation's citizenry. It's the stuff upon which many of world history's wars and revolutions have been based.

Democratic governance, especially one based upon the principles of an elected representation exercising the will of the people, is a delicate ideology to balance in light of the greed and avaricious influences common in the practice of capitalism and a free market economy. An elected representative holds the power of the people. When some choose to act in their interests, or those of special interests, often motivated by personal profit, they do so in ways contrary to the people's will. When this happens, a genuine danger exists to our liberty and freedoms. In our nation's future, we might need to replace our current representative democracy with a true democracy. It may become essential to adopt a one-citizen, one-vote form of democracy instead of our current practice of democracy as a republic practiced today.

It must be noted that the United States is also known as a "republic," meaning it's a form of government in which the people hold power and exercise it through their elected representatives. In a republic, the people elect representatives to make decisions on their behalf, and the representatives represent the people's interests. This governmental system balances the people's power with the need for effective decision-making and governance, hypothetically.

The United States form of representative democracy combines the principles of democracy, where the people have a say in the decisions that affect their lives, with the principles of a republic, where elected representatives exercise political power on behalf of the people. This form of democracy allows the United States to have a government that's responsive to the needs and desires of the people while also providing a stable and effective system of governance. However, capitalism has become a solid deterrent to its effectiveness in modern times.

History tells us that ancient Rome was a republic, unlike ancient Athens, which was a democracy. After overthrowing its monarchy, Rome developed a republican system of government where citizens elected officials to make decisions for the public. That's the core of how the U.S. government works.

Historically, the terms 'democracy' and 'republic' have been presented as opposing concepts. However, in reality, they share significant similarities. The ancient Greek democracy established in Athens was a direct democracy rather than a representative democracy. Any adult male citizen over 20 had the right and responsibility to participate directly in the decision-making process. This system partially elected officials through the Assembly and partly chose them through a process called "sortition," which was a lottery.

In a direct democracy, citizens make decisions directly, without intermediaries such as elected representatives. Sortition is a selection method that uses a random drawing to choose individuals for a particular role or task. Sortion uses various means, such as drawing names from a hat or using a computer program to select individuals from a list randomly.

In the United States, sortition is most commonly used to select prospective jurors for criminal trials. In common-law systems, juries are an integral part of the legal process, and their role is to determine the facts of a case and apply the law as instructed by the judge. Juries are randomly selected from the pool of potential jurors to ensure that they represent the community. This system helps to prevent bias and ensures that the legal system is fair and impartial.

Sortition is also sometimes used to form citizen groups with political advisory power. These groups, known as citizens assemblies or citizens juries, are made up of individuals who are randomly selected to represent the broader population. Sortion typically tasks groups with examining a particular issue or problem and providing recommendations or advice to policymakers.

According to some, randomly selecting individuals may not result in choosing the most qualified or knowledgeable citizens for a particular role. Others argue sortition could be a more democratic and fair method of selection, as it helps prevent the influence of special interests or other factors that might skew the selection process.

Sortition, a method of selection used for centuries in various contexts, including U.S. governance and the choice of jurors in common-law systems, continues to be applied today. While it has critics, it's essential for ensuring fairness and impartiality in many decision-making processes.

The Roman Republic originally had a system of government based on representative democracy, in which citizens elected representatives to make decisions on their behalf. However, power shifted away from this system and toward a centralized imperial authority over time, with the emperor holding the most political power. This transition marked the Roman Republic's end and the Roman Empire's beginning, characterized by a strong, centralized imperial authority rather than a system of representative democracy. This change is sometimes called a "blueprint for the future of [our] American democracy."

In practice, "republic" and "representative democracy" are often used interchangeably to describe the same political system. Representative democracy is a form of democracy, just as the "Granny Smith" apple is a form of an apple. Therefore it is accurate to refer to the United States as a "democracy," following the examples of scholars such as Thomas Jefferson, John Adams, Noah Webster, and Chief Justice John Marshall, as mentioned earlier. The United States is also a "republic," a term used to describe a system of government where power is held by elected representatives rather than the people directly. This description is accurate for the United States too.

The choice of terminology between "representative democracy" and "republic" is often a matter of personal preference and political inference. It's far more important to focus on ensuring that the U.S. government represents the needs and interests of the people, regardless of the specific term used to describe the system of government.

The U.S. can be most precisely and accurately described as a "federal constitutional representative democracy" or a "federal constitutional republic." Specific features reflected in these terms most accurately describe the United States of America.

The U.S. government has a Constitution that was drafted to restrict its power. The Constitution cedes that restricted power to the people and their representatives. This document defines a federal system of government that divides power between a national government and regional and local governments. Additionally, it establishes a system of representative democracy in which citizens elect representatives to make decisions on their behalf.

While using more specific terms to describe the U.S. government is accurate, it's not always necessary to be so precise. As stated, the words "democracy" and "republic" are often used interchangeably to refer to the American system of government for this reason.

In a literal sense, the United States is still a democracy and a republic, as it's a system of government in which power is held by the people, either directly or through their elected representatives. However, many are concerned about the current "functioning" of this form of democracy in the United States.

In 2016, The Economist Intelligence Unit (EIU) downgraded the United States from a "full democracy" to a "flawed democracy" in its "Democracy Index" (Economic Intelligence Unit, 2016), citing declining trust in government as one of the main reasons for the downgrade. There are several other reasons why the EIU cited falling trust in government for the downgrade from a "full democracy" to a "flawed democracy."

One is that trust in government has been declining in the United States for many years. Another study by the Pew Research Center found that confidence in the federal government was highest in the 1960s, with approximately three-quarters of Americans expressing confidence in the government. This study indicated trust in the government has declined since then, and as of 2016, only about a quarter of Americans expressed confidence in their federal government.

The EIU cited declining trust in government as another reason for the downgrade because trust in government indicates a functioning of democracy. Low trust in government causes people to be less likely to believe government hears their voices and is meeting their needs. Declining trust can lead to disillusionment and disengagement from the democratic process. This circumstance can negatively affect the democratic process, which can negatively affect the functioning of democracy. Specifically, this disengagement is globally discouraging the electorate's participation in the democratic process, resulting in them not participating in elections. This lack of involvement can skew the perception of "the will of the people" by its elected representatives.

There are also other specific examples of how declining trust in government can empirically impact the functioning of democracy in the United States. For example, low trust in government can lead to low voter turnout, as people might feel their votes don't matter or that the government isn't responsive to their needs. Lacking trust in government can also lead to the erosion of civil liberties, as people could be more willing to accept restrictions on their freedom in exchange for greater security.

The EIU downgraded the United States from a "full democracy" to a "flawed democracy" in its "Democracy Index" due to declining trust in government, which has had negative consequences for the functioning of our democracy. This declining trust has been a trend in the U.S. for many years.

In 2021, the "International Institute for Democracy and Electoral Assistance" also classified the United States as a "backsliding democracy" for the first time. This classification means that the United States is seen as a democracy, regressing or deteriorating somehow.

These evaluations suggest that while the United States may be a democracy and a republic in theory, there are issues with how these principles are practically applied. For example, elected representatives may not truly represent the people's interests.

Qualified Privilege

The political franchise or a citizen's "right" to vote is not absolute in the United States. The U.S. Constitution denies citizens the right to vote in certain circumstances. For example, voting rights are typically restricted to citizens 18 or older because it's believed that individuals who are not yet adults are not fully capable of making informed decisions and participating in the democratic process.

In addition to age, certain criminal convictions can also disqualify an individual from voting. For example, some States may deny voting rights to individuals serving a prison sentence or on parole or probation. Some deny voting right to all convicted felons, regardless of the satisfaction of their sentences. U.S. society often imposes these restrictions based on the belief that people convicted of a crime and serving a sentence have demonstrated a lack of respect for the laws and values of society; therefore, they are not allowed to participate in the democratic process.

More than 3.5 million U.S. citizens still did not have the right to vote for the U.S. President in the most recent 2020 national election. This situation exists because these Americans are officially considered citizens of U.S. territories, which coincidentally are also predominantly populated by racial or ethnic minorities. They don't have the right to vote due to their residential locations and the U.S. constitutionally-defined status of their specific geographic territory.

While the Democratic and Republican National Committees allow territorial citizens to participate in the nomination of Presidential candidates, and residents of U.S. territories can vote for nonvoting delegates in the U.S. House of Representatives, they don't have any voting representation in Congress. This policy means citizens in the U.S. Virgin Islands, Puerto Rico, Guam, the Northern Mariana Islands, or American Samoa cannot have a say in Congress about decisions that affect them. This policy means even though Congress has absolute and complete authority over their territorial matters, they have no representative voice in Congress. On the surface, it's a matter of trust that Congress will always act positively considering territorial interests. In actuality, nothing could be further from the truth. The territorial authority of Congress, absent any elected territorial representation therein, essentially makes the U.S. Congress a dictatorial body governing the U.S. insular territories. This dictatorship is a fact of U.S. law, albeit rarely stated.

Residents of U.S. territories, such as the U.S. Virgin Islands, Puerto Rico, Guam, the Northern Mariana Islands, and American Samoa, can vote for nonvoting delegates in the U.S. House of Representatives. Still, they don't have voting representation in Congress. These citizens cannot elect Congressional members or participate in the legislative process like U.S. citizens of States do.

The U.S. Commission on Civil Rights report to Congress (October 2021), titled "Voting Rights in U.S. Territories," cites, "An often-overlooked way in which citizens of the U.S., primarily those from traditionally marginalized communities, are denied the right to vote is through the deprivation of the right to vote to residents of U.S. territories." The report states, "Based solely on place of residence, Americans who live in the territories are denied voting representation in either house of Congress, even though Congress possesses plenary authority over local, territorial matters." In a sense, U.S. citizens living in a U.S. territory don't live in either a genuinely representative democracy or a republic for this reason.

The reason residents of territories cannot vote for Congress members or have full voting representation in Congress is that territories aren't fully sovereign states. Therefore their residents don't have the same rights and privileges as citizens in the States. Under the U.S. Constitution, Congress has complete authority over territorial matters and has the power to determine the rights and benefits of the residents of U.S. territories, including extending their citizens not only the right to vote but also to grant them voting representation in Congress.

Unfortunately, citizens living in these territories cannot have a say in decisions that affect them because Congress has complete authority over their territorial matters. Historically, Congress has not relinquished its jurisdiction over the territories in favor of representative democracy. Ironically, the very body of our democratic representation denies representative democracy to more than 3.5 million U.S. citizens.

These fellow Americans don't have the exact representation in Congress as other citizens in the States. This disqualification means territorial citizens are disenfranchised and have no voice in many decisions affecting their lives. It also means Congress governs them, a governmental power never extended to Congress or intended by the original U.S. Constitution. They have no democratic option to choose Congressional representation. In a representative democracy, citizens elect representatives to make decisions. Federal elected representation is not the case for more than 3.5 million U.S. citizens.

In addition to the 50 States and the District of Columbia, the United States territories are islands and unincorporated areas in the Caribbean Sea and the Pacific Ocean that the U.S. federal government controls. U.S. territories include Puerto Rico, Guam, the Northern Mariana Islands, American Samoa, and Minor Outlying Islands.

People born in the 50 States, the District of Columbia, or the four significant territories of Puerto Rico, the U.S. Virgin Islands, Guam, and the Northern Mariana Islands are U.S. citizens. Interestingly, American Samoa is an unincorporated territory of the United States, which means that it's subject to the authority of the U.S. government. However, its residents are still considered "conditional" U.S. citizens.

People born in American Samoa are U.S. nationals but not U.S. citizens like people born in the 50 states. Samoans are afforded certain rights and protections under U.S. law but are not entitled to all the rights and privileges of U.S. citizenship. For example, U.S. nationals cannot vote in federal elections, and they may not be able to travel as quickly to and from the United States as U.S. citizens can. However, U.S. nationals can apply for U.S. citizenship through naturalization.

American Samoa's status can confuse some people as a territory of the United States. It is subject to the laws and regulations of the U.S. However, the legal status of American Samoa is different from that of other insular territories, affecting the rights and privileges of those born there.

The reason why those born in American Samoa are considered U.S. nationals rather than citizens is American Samoa's unique territorial status. Unlike Puerto Rico or the U.S. Virgin Islands, in the case of American Samoa, the U.S. didn't acquire it through treaty or conquest. Instead, American Samoa is under the jurisdiction of the United States through a series of agreements with the Samoan islands and is considered a different type of U.S. territory.

This status can be a source of frustration for many people living in American Samoa, as they cannot fully participate in the democratic process and don't have the exact representation in Congress as citizens living in the States, among other things. A caveat is their legal status does allow for flexibility in the rights and privileges afforded to those born there and the possibility of further integration into the United States.

The territories of Puerto Rico, the U.S. Virgin Islands, Guam, and the Northern Mariana Islands are all subject to the plenary power of Congress, which means that Congress has the authority to make laws for these territories and to override any regulations made by their local governments. However, the residents of these territories don't have the right to vote in federal elections and don't have representation in Congress. This policy is because these territories aren't States within the United States and don't have the same political autonomy as the States.

The United States doesn't incorporate the other territories, so they don't have the right to vote either. Incorporation is the process of a region becoming a state, fully integrated into the U.S. political and legal systems. The territories of Puerto Rico, the U.S. Virgin Islands, Guam, and the Northern Mariana Islands haven't undergone this process. They, therefore, don't have the same political rights and responsibilities as the States.

The District of Columbia, also known as "Washington D.C.," serves as the U.S. federal capital and, as such, is a unique federal district rather than a State. As a result, it doesn't have voting representation in Congress either. The Constitution grants Congress exclusive jurisdiction over the District of Columbia. In the House of Representatives, Washington D.C. has a delegate who cannot vote on the House floor but can participate in voting on procedural matters and in congressional committees. D.C. residents don't have any representation in the Senate.

The 23rd Amendment, adopted in 1961, gives D.C. the same number of electoral votes as the least populous State in the Presidential and Vice-Presidential elections. The 23rd Amendment also grants citizens of Washington, D.C., the right to vote in presidential elections. Before this amendment, residents of the District could not participate in the presidential electoral process, even though they were required to pay federal taxes and were subject to the laws and regulations of the federal government.

Electors to the electoral college from Washington D.C. count when tallying the total vote count for President. The District of Columbia (D.C.) is treated as a state for purposes of the electoral college and has the same number of electors as the least populous state, which is currently three. Electors from D.C. participate in the electoral college process with the 50 states, and their votes count the same as the states.

As stated, the 23rd Amendment grants the District of Columbia three electors in the Electoral College, the same number of electors as the least populous State. These electors are chosen similarly to those in the 50 States. They must cast their electoral votes for the Presidential and Vice-Presidential candidates who receive the most votes in the federal district. The U.S. electoral college is used to elect the President and Vice President.

Considering the number of individuals denied the voting privilege of U.S. citizenship and the low voter turnout among eligible citizens, it becomes clear that voter participation in the United States does not accurately reflect a "representative democracy" or that of a "representative republic."

Meanwhile, voters cast ballots for their preferred candidates in a U.S. presidential election. The polls are counted, and the candidate who receives the most votes in a state wins that state's electoral votes. The U.S. determines the number of each state's electoral votes by its population. For example, California has the largest population and electoral votes (55).

The vote count is determined, and the candidate who has won the most electoral votes is declared the election's winner. In most cases, the electoral college winner also wins the popular vote (i.e., the most votes from the general public). However, this is not always the case. In 2000 and 2016, the candidate who won the electoral college didn't win the popular vote.

The Founders chose an electoral college system to balance power between the small and large states. Under the plan, each state gets a certain number of electoral votes, regardless of size. The electoral college system means that smaller states have a more significant influence on the outcome of the election, as they have a disproportionate number of electoral votes compared to their population.

The U.S. electoral college is integral to the U.S. presidential election process. It ensures that all states are represented in the election and helps balance the power between the small and large states.

This system is contradictory to D.C., despite its having three electors. Having a non-voting member in Congress means the people of the District of Columbia don't have Congressional representation, regardless of their number of electors. However, the District does influence the outcome of a Presidential election through its three electors, even though its citizens have no significant influence or voting representation in Congress.

While the 23rd Amendment has helped to improve citizen voting rights in the District of Columbia, it doesn't grant them representation. Washington, D.C., is not a State. For this reason, District residents don't have a direct say in the federal laws and policies that affect them, only in who will be the two elected members of the Executive branch, president and vice-president.

Despite these limitations, the 23rd Amendment has significantly impacted citizens' voting rights in the District of

Columbia. It's allowed them to at least participate in the presidential electoral process fully and have a limited voice in selecting the nation's leaders.

Most recently, the District of Columbia has made compelling arguments for U.S. Statehood. Unlike residents of the U.S. territories such as Puerto Rico or Guam, who also have non-voting delegates in Congress, the citizens of the District of Columbia pay all U.S. federal taxes. In the fiscal year 2007 alone, D.C. residents and businesses paid $20.4 billion in federal taxes, more than the taxes collected from 19 states. That year, this amount also represented the nation's highest federal taxes per capita.

It's argued that the District of Columbia is the only place within the United States where citizens are required to fulfill the responsibilities of citizenship, such as paying taxes and registering for the Selective Service, without having the full rights and privileges of citizenship. This denial of total voting rights makes it a unique political and geographical entity within the country. The District has the responsibilities of a State without enjoying all the rights and privileges provided for in the U.S. Constitution. D.C.'s situation has often been referred to throughout U.S. history as "taxation without representation." This belief is also the district's motto now printed on its motor vehicle license plates.

The U.S. territories have varying levels of autonomy, but they're all subject to US law. Each region has its unique history and culture, making them a diverse part of the United States

Some of the nation's States may have additional requirements or restrictions on voting, such as proof of residence or citizenship, that can disqualify specific individuals. These requirements typically have been put in place to ensure the integrity of the voting process. They also prevent fraud. However, state requirements regarding voting rights remain controversial. Several legal challenges have recently been based on State voting requirements. In succeeding chapters, we'll explore some of them.

Importance of the Right

The right to vote is an essential aspect of any democracy, yet in the U.S., again, it's not absolute. Prevailing U.S. law denies the franchise or privilege of voting based on certain circumstances. Yet the right to vote is also the cornerstone of a true democracy, as voting allows citizens to have a say in the decisions affecting their lives and communities. It's a fundamental right that ensures all members of society have an equal opportunity to participate in the political process.

Voting is crucial because it allows citizens to hold their elected representatives accountable. When people can vote, they can choose leaders who reflect their values and priorities and hold those leaders responsible for their actions once they're in office. This participation helps create a system of checks and balances essential for maintaining a healthy democracy.

Another reason the right to vote is crucial is that it allows for diverse viewpoints. A true democracy makes decisions by considering all voices and perspectives. By enabling every citizen to vote, the political system can more accurately reflect the will of all the nation's people and consider the needs and concerns of all members of our society.

In addition, the right to vote helps to promote equality and fairness in the political process. It ensures that everyone has an equal say in the decisions that affect their lives, regardless of their social or economic status. This right helps to prevent the concentration of power in the hands of a select few and promotes a more inclusive and representative government.

When people feel that their vote matters and that they have a say in the decisions that affect their lives, they're more likely to become engaged in the political process and advocate for the issues that matter to them. This participation helps create a more vibrant and engaged citizenry, which is essential for the health and stability of any democratic society.

Voting is a vital component of our U.S. democracy. This right allows citizens to hold their elected representatives accountable, express diverse viewpoints, promote equality and fairness in the political process, and encourage active participation. Without this fundamental right, U.S. democracy can't function effectively. We would be unable to meet the needs and concerns of all members of our society. Ironically, this has historically been true in the U.S. We have persistently failed to meet the needs and concerns of all citizens.

Suffrage, also known as the right to vote, is a fundamental principle of democracy. It ensures that all citizens of a country have an equal right to participate in the political process through voting. In addition to the practice of voter suppression, due to the denial of U.S. voting rights to all of its citizens, the U.S. cannot be defined as a truly representative democracy, as millions of our U.S. citizens have no representation in the federal government.

Voting right in the U.S. has been a critical issue throughout history, with various groups fighting for and sometimes being denied voting based on age, race, gender, property ownership, or geographic location. Through ongoing activism and struggle, U.S. citizens continue to strive for their right to vote. Absent universal voting rights of its citizenry, the U.S. isn't a truly representative democracy. Even though the right to vote is vital to U.S. citizenship, it has almost exclusively been the one most universally denied by our government throughout history.

Suffrage Through Amendments

The United States Constitution, adopted in 1787, didn't extend the right to vote to all citizens. The Constitution only gave that right to white men who owned property. Excluded from the political process were women, people of color, poor white men, and all U.S. citizen children. As a side note, like the enslaved, in many ways throughout U.S. history, children were treated more like property than individuals with all citizenship rights. Meanwhile, this provision granting the right to vote to white men who were property owners was in the original draft of our Constitution. A series of amendments and legislation at the federal and state levels extended the privilege of voting, often termed "a right," to more and more groups of people over time.

The mention of gender rights in the U.S. Constitution is a hotly debated topic. The granting of voting rights to white male property owners is often discussed relative to gender because it excluded women from voting based on gender. However, technically speaking, the U.S. Constitution does not explicitly mention gender in this context. It is argued that the relevant gender-specific text is found in the 14th Amendment to the Constitution, ratified in 1868, well after the founding documents of the United States.

The 14th Amendment grants citizenship to all persons born or naturalized in the United States and prohibits states from denying any person equal protection of the laws. While this amendment does not explicitly mention gender, it has been used in cases related to gender discrimination, such as in the landmark case of Reed v. Reed (1971), which established that gender discrimination violates the Equal Protection Clause of the Fourteenth Amendment.

The 14th Amendment, adopted in 1868, first mentions gender in this context by stating the following: "All persons born or naturalized in the United States, and subject to the jurisdiction thereof, are citizens of the United States and of the State wherein they reside. No State shall make or enforce any law which shall abridge the privileges or immunities of citizens of the United States; nor shall any State deprive any person of life, liberty, or property, without due process of law; nor deny to any person within its jurisdiction the equal protection of the laws." Our Courts interpreted this to mean all male citizens over 21 have the right to vote. The 14th Amendment then extended voting rights to all white men. The amendment didn't grant women voting rights and essentially denied them the vote until the passage of the 19th Amendment in 1920. This fact is also essential when discussing voting rights in the United States.

The 15th Amendment, adopted in 1870, granted the right to vote to African-American men, while the 19th Amendment, adopted in 1920, granted the right to vote to women. In the U.S., formerly enslaved African-American men were granted the right to vote before the nation's women. The 26th Amendment was adopted in 1971. This Amendment lowered the voting age for all citizens from 21 to 18. Effectively, this extended voting right to all adults since 18 is the age established by the government as the beginning of a U.S. citizen's adulthood, at least in terms of extending the franchise, or privilege, of voting.

Today, voting is fundamental in the U.S., and all adult citizens who are 18 years or older, residing in the 50 States, and not felons, are eligible to vote. Many U.S. citizens today still don't enjoy equal protection under the law or the extension of the right to vote. The U.S. also continues to exclude its citizen children from voting.

In recent years, there have been efforts in some U.S. states to pass laws that make it more difficult for certain groups of people, such as low-income or minority voters, to access the polls. These measures, which include voter identification requirements and limitations on early voting, have been challenged in court as violating the voting rights of qualified citizens.

In 2011, Texas passed a voter identification law requiring voters to present one of several forms of government-issued photo ID to vote. Civil rights groups challenged this law in court, who argued that it would disproportionately affect minority and low-income voters, who are less likely to have the required identification. A federal court in 2017 determined that a voter identification law passed in Texas disproportionately affected minority voters and mandated modifications to it, including the types of acceptable forms of identification.

In 2013, North Dakota passed a law requiring voters to present proof of their residential address to vote. This law was challenged in court by the Native American Rights Fund, which argued that it would disproportionately affect Native American voters, who are less likely to have a residential address or the required forms of identification. A federal court struck down the law in 2018.

In addition, multiple states reduced early voting days. For example, in Georgia, where a law was passed in 2019 reducing early voting days from 21 to 17, a Federal court later ruled that it discriminated against African American voters.

These are just a few examples of the efforts in some U.S. states to pass laws that make it more difficult for certain groups of people to access the polls, and they demonstrate the ongoing struggle to protect the voting rights of all citizens in the country.

Voter ID laws and a limit on early voting aim to prevent voter fraud. Still, ensuring they do not discriminate against specific groups and violate constitutional voting rights is crucial, especially for low-income and minority voters. There should be a balance between preventing voter fraud and preserving voter rights.

There have also been efforts in some States to pass laws that make it more difficult for certain groups of people, such as low-income or minority voters, to access the polls. Courts have challenged voter identification requirements and limitations on early voting included in rules for violating the principle of suffrage, claiming that such measures infringe upon a person's right to cast their vote.

Despite these challenges, voting right remains a cornerstone of representative democracy, as it's practiced in the United States. Through voting, citizens can have a say in who represents them and what policies affect their communities. Genuine universal suffrage is a crucial component of a fair and just democratic society, and it's up to all citizens to demand, defend and protect this fundamental right.

Chapter 2

Owning the Franchise

The United States Constitution, adopted in 1787, didn't initially grant the right to vote to all citizens. Instead, voting was limited to white men who owned property. The nation's founders limited the right to vote based on their beliefs and values. They reasoned that only white men who owned land had a stake in society and the necessary knowledge and judgment to make informed decisions about the country's direction. The writers of the U.S. Constitution wrote it during a time when their land was primarily agricultural. Thus the Founders believed only property owners had a stake in the community's well-being. They also believed that only white men were capable of rational thought and fit to participate in the political process.

The founders limited the franchise privilege to vote for several reasons. One of these reasons was the political climate of the time. Many founders held skepticism towards democracy, believing that restricting the right to vote would prevent the majority from exerting power over the minority. This determination influenced their decision to limit the right to vote. They also believed that a narrow franchise would ensure that the government was comprised of the most qualified and capable individuals.

Despite these justifications, the limited franchise was ultimately a belief in the superiority of white men and the exclusion of other groups from the political process. This belief was rooted in the country's history of slavery and discrimination. It would take significant social and political changes – including the abolition of slavery, granting citizenship to African-Americans, and the movement for women's suffrage – to challenge and eventually change this exclusionary system.

The founding fathers of the United States were also concerned about the possibility of a direct democracy, in which the opinions of the general public could become law directly because they feared that the ordinary person's views might not be well-informed or well-reasoned. As a result, they established an indirect form of democracy, a "representative democracy" or a "republic," in which elected officials represent the general public's opinions. The founding fathers hoped to ensure that the country's laws were based on more thoughtful and considered judgment by limiting the right to vote in this way.

Articles of Confederation and Constitution

The "United States Constitution" is the supreme law and the U.S. federal government's foundation. It was drafted in 1787 by a group of 55 delegates to the Constitutional Convention in Philadelphia, Pennsylvania, and it took effect on March 4, 1789.

The U.S. Constitution was drafted in response to weaknesses of the "Articles of Confederation," serving as the first form of a national government in the United States after the American Revolution. The Articles of Confederation established a central government with limited powers, and the States retained significant autonomy and sovereignty. This system had proven inadequate in dealing with the young nation's challenges, including trade, foreign relations, and national defense.

The Articles of Confederation served as the country's governing document from 1781 to 1789. They were written in the aftermath of the American Revolution, as the newly independent States sought to create a system of government that would unite them in a common cause while preserving their sovereignty and independence.

The Articles of Confederation established a central government with limited powers, giving the States significant autonomy and sovereignty. The national government was a unicameral legislature called the "Continental Congress," which had the authority to declare war, make peace, and conduct foreign relations. However, Congress had no power to levy taxes or regulate commerce, and it was dependent on the States for funding.

The Articles of Confederation lacked a robust and centralized government authority. The national government had no power to enforce its laws or regulate the States, leading to many problems, including trade and foreign relations disputes. The States also had difficulty working together and often acted in their self-interest, leading to a lack of cooperation and unity.

In 1787, the U.S. called a Constitutional Convention to address problems and create a more effective government. George Washington presided over the Constitutional Convention, which representatives from each of the 13 States attended. The delegates to the Convention drafted a new plan of government that would be more effective and better suited to the nation's needs.

The Constitution they ultimately adopted resulted from extensive debate and compromise among the delegates. The document established a federal system at the Constitutional Convention, balancing national and state powers. The U.S. Constitution also established three branches of government: the legislative, executive, and judicial. This separation of powers prevents any unit from gaining too much power and is a vital feature of the U.S. government. This separation ensures the balance between the three areas of government. A system of checks and balances helps safeguard individual liberties and maintain a balance of power within the government, making it a critical feature of the U.S. government today.

Establishing Branches

The United States Constitution established three branches of government: the legislative, executive, and judicial. These branches function together as a system of checks and balances, ensuring that no one unit becomes too powerful. The founding fathers saw this system of separation of powers as a necessary way to prevent tyranny and protect the rights and freedoms of citizens.

The legislative branch of government is responsible for making laws. It comprises two houses: the Senate and the House of Representatives. Members of Congress elected by the people serve fixed terms. The U.S. assigns two senators from each state to the Senate and determines the number of House Representatives from each state based on its population. The legislative branch levies taxes, regulates commerce and can declare war. It also has the power to impeach and remove officials from office. Members of the U.S. Senate serve six years, and U.S. House of Representatives members serve for two years.

The executive branch of government is responsible for enforcing the laws. The people elect the President, who serves as the head of the government for a term of four years. The President has the power to veto laws passed by Congress and to make treaties with foreign countries. The President also serves as the military's commander-in-chief and is responsible for the administration of the government. The executive branch also includes the Vice President, who serves as the President's deputy and assumes the presidency in the event of the President's death, resignation, or removal from office.

The judicial branch of government is responsible for interpreting the laws and constitution. The judiciary is a system of federal courts, including the Supreme Court, the highest court in the land. The judicial branch can interpret the Constitution and determine the constitutionality of laws and government actions. It also can resolve disputes between the States, individuals, and the government.

Judges serve for life or until they retire or are removed from office in the U.S. judicial branch, including the federal courts and the

Supreme Court, to which they're appointed. Federal judges are appointed by the President and confirmed by the Senate. Congress impeaches and removes judges from office, or they retire or resign.

The Chief Justice of the Supreme Court and the other justices of the Supreme Court are also appointed by the President and confirmed by the Senate, and they serve during good behavior. This lifetime appointment system ensures the judicial branch's independence and protects the judges from political pressure.

Courts are Organized

The federal court system in the United States has three levels: the district courts, the courts of appeals, and the Supreme Court. Each plays an essential role in the judicial branch of government.

District courts are the trial courts of the federal court system and are the first level of the federal judiciary. There are 94 district courts in the United States, one for each State, the District of Columbia, and several territories. The district courts have jurisdiction over a wide range of federal cases, including criminal cases, civil cases, and bankruptcy cases.

The courts of appeals are the intermediate level of the federal court system and are responsible for reviewing decisions made by the district courts. There are 13 courts of Appeals in the United States, each covering a specific geographic region. The appeals courts can hear appeals from the district courts and review federal agencies' decisions.

The Supreme Court is the highest in the land and is the final level of the federal court system. The Supreme Court has nine justices, including the Chief Justice, and its authority is to review decisions made by the lower federal and state courts. The Supreme Court has the final say on federal law and the Constitution, and its decisions are binding on all other courts in the United States.

The federal court system is hierarchical, with the district courts at the bottom, the courts of appeals in the middle, and the Supreme Court at the top. This structure allows a review of legal decisions made at each level of the system and helps to ensure that the law is applied consistently throughout the country.

Each of the three branches of government works together as a system of checks and balances. Each department has certain powers and responsibilities, and they're all accountable to one another. For example, Congress can impeach and remove officials from office, while the judicial branch can interpret the Constitution and determine the constitutionality of laws. This separation of powers helps prevent any unit from gaining too much power and ensures that the government is accountable to the people.

Overall, the founding fathers saw the establishment of the three branches of government as a necessary way to prevent tyranny and protect the rights and freedoms of citizens. The system of separation of powers has played a crucial role in the development of the United States. It continues to be a vital part of the American system of government.

The Articles of Confederation were the basis for the U.S. Constitution and played a crucial role in the early development of the United States. However, weaknesses led to the drafting of the Constitution, which created a more effective and responsive form of government for the nation. The Constitution has played a vital role in the historical development of the United States, and it continues to be a fundamental part of the American system of government.

The Constitution that was ultimately adopted resulted from extensive debate and compromise among the delegates. The document formally established a federal system of government with the powers of the national government carefully balanced with those of the States. The U.S. Constitution's establishment of the three branches of government: the legislative, executive, and judicial, remains a core feature of the document to this day. The separation of powers established by the document has significantly impacted the United States' growth. It remains a vital aspect of the American system of government.

A Bill of Rights

One of the most critical parts of the Constitution is the Bill of Rights, the first ten of twenty-seven amendments. The U.S. added amendments to the Constitution in response to concerns that it didn't adequately protect the rights and freedoms of citizens. The Bill of Rights guarantees the right to freedom of speech, religion, and the press, the right to bear arms, and the right to a fair and speedy trial.

The U.S. Bill of Rights is a vital part of the American system of government. The Bill of Rights was added in 1791, a few years after the Constitution's ratification. The ten articles guarantee American citizens fundamental rights and freedoms, including freedom of speech, religion, and the press, the right to bear arms, and a fair and speedy trial.

One of the most critical aspects of the Bill of Rights is that it limits the government's powers and protects individuals' rights. The Bill of Rights prohibits the government from infringing certain rights and limits its ability to search and seize private property. This prohibition prevents abuses of power and ensures that the government is accountable to the people.

The Bill of Rights is also a cornerstone of American democracy and the Rule of Law. It helps to ensure that the government is transparent and accountable and provides a framework for protecting individual rights.

These first 10 Amendments to the U.S. Constitution guarantee American citizens fundamental rights and freedoms. They limit the powers of the government and protect the rights of individuals. The Bill of Rights is both a critical part of the American system of government and an essential component of the U.S. Constitution.

The United States founders wrote the Constitution to establish a more effective and responsive government. The document shows a federal system of government that balances the powers of the national government with those of the States, and it sets a system of checks and balances to ensure that no one branch of government becomes too powerful. The Constitution has played a crucial role in the development of the United States throughout the centuries, and it continues to be the guiding spirit behind the American system of government.

As the United States changed and evolved, the restricted voting franchise became perceived as increasingly unjust. The Industrial Revolution brought about significant changes in the U.S. economy and society. The growth of cities and the rise of a new urban working class challenged the idea that only property owners should have the right to vote.

Revolution in Industry

The Industrial Revolution in the U.S. significantly impacted voting rights in the country. The Industrial Revolution, which started in the late 18th century and stretched to the 19th century, initiated significant changes in the production of goods, the economy, and society. One of the consequences of the Industrial Revolution was the growth of urbanization, as more and more people migrated from rural areas to cities in search of work. This consequence led to the development of a new class of factory workers, who often worked long hours in poor conditions for low wages. Many of these workers were recent immigrants or members of minority groups, and they often faced discrimination and exclusion from the political process.

Another consequence of the Industrial Revolution was the expansion of suffrage, or the right to vote. During this time, many States began to eliminate property qualifications for voting, which had previously restricted the franchise to white male property owners. This elimination led to an expansion of the voting rights of white men, but it didn't extend to women or people of color.

In addition to these changes, the Industrial Revolution also contributed to the rise of political parties and interest groups, which played a crucial role in shaping the political landscape of the United States. These Parties and interest groups often focused on issues related to the Industrial Revolution, such as labor rights and economic policy. They played a significant role in shaping the government's policy decisions.

The Industrial Revolution significantly impacted voting rights. It also played a crucial role in shaping the country's political landscape by spawning political Parties and specific interest groups determined to advocate for their particular issues and interests.

As stated, the abolition of slavery and granting citizenship to African-Americans after the Civil War raised questions about the fairness of denying the right to vote to a large portion of the male population based on race. These developments, along with the growing movement for women's suffrage, led to calls for the general expansion of the voting franchise.

The Civil War marked a significant turning point in the history of the United States, as it brought an end to the practice of slavery and laid the foundation for a more equal and just society. However, despite the abolition of slavery and the adoption of the 13th, 14th, and 15th Amendments, which granted African-Americans citizenship, equal protection under the law, and the right to vote, the nation still struggled with racial inequality and discrimination.

A significant question after the Civil War was whether denying the right to vote to a large portion of the male population based on race was fair. The 15th Amendment, which granted African-American men the right to vote, was a significant step toward equality and justice. Still, it didn't go far enough in addressing the systemic barriers to voting that continued to affect African-Americans disproportionately. Individuals and state authorities implemented obstacles, for example, literacy tests, poll taxes, and other methods, to prevent African-Americans from casting their votes. In addition to the growing movement for civil rights, there was also a growing movement for women's suffrage. Women, who made up a significant portion of the population, had long been denied the right to vote and were excluded from participating in the political process. The suffrage movement, which gained momentum in the late 19th and early 20th centuries, sought to expand the voting franchise to include the nation's women.

The combination of two movements, with other developments such as the rise of the progressive movement and increasing recognition of the importance of universal suffrage, led to calls for the expansion of the voting franchise. These calls were eventually successful, as the 19th Amendment, which granted women the right to vote, was ratified in 1920.

The questions raised after the Civil War about the fairness of denying the right to vote to a large portion of the male population and the growing movement for women's suffrage played a significant role in expanding the voting franchise. These efforts helped create a more inclusive and representative democracy and have had a lasting impact on the political landscape of the United States.

Amendments Expanding

As a result of calls for expansion, a series of amendments to the Constitution were adopted, extending the right to vote to more and more groups of people. As discussed earlier, the 14th Amendment, adopted in 1868, first mentions gender in the Constitution by stating that all male citizens over 21 have the right to vote. This amendment extended voting rights to all white men. The 15th Amendment, adopted in 1870, granted the right to vote to African-American men, while the 19th Amendment, adopted in 1920, granted the right to vote to women. The 26th Amendment, adopted in 1971, lowered the voting age from 21 to 18, effectively giving the right to vote to all adult citizens. Yet, all voting rights Amendments remain Constitutionally conditioned to discriminate against citizens by age, geographic location, and felon status.

Changes were made in voting rights reflected by the understanding that the right to vote should not depend on factors such as race, gender, or property ownership. Instead, they should be universal and equally available to all citizens – except citizen children, citizens residing in specific locations, and felons. The latter three groups constitute nearly a third of the U.S. population. Think about that for a moment.

At the same time, there have been ongoing challenges and efforts to restrict the right to vote for certain groups of people, reverse voting progress, and abridge the principle of genuine universal suffrage. That "voting" cornerstone of democracy remains elusive in the so-called "representative democracy" of the United States, even today.

Urban working-class white men played a crucial role in challenging the idea that only white male property owners should have the right to vote. This change was a significant achievement because, before voting rights expanded, only a tiny minority of white men could participate in the political process. By challenging this restrictive system, these men helped to ensure that all citizens had a voice in their government and could shape the policies that impacted their lives.

Individuals and groups in the United States challenged the requirement that one had to own property to be able to vote as the country became more industrialized and urbanized. As people migrated to cities searching for work, they faced various social, economic, and political challenges different from their rural counterparts. Many urban working-class white men struggled to make ends meet and were frustrated by the lack of representation they had in government. Sound familiar?

To address these issues, working-class white men began organizing and advocating for political reform. They formed labor unions, political Parties, and other organizations to push for changes that would give them a more significant say in the decisions that affected their lives. These efforts often involved political activism.

Lobbying lawmakers, protesting, and engaging in other forms of civil disobedience were all ways urban working-class white men attempted to bring about social and political change. These forms of activism effectively drew attention to issues and influenced decision-makers, but they were also controversial and divisive.

Lobbying activity attempts to influence decisions made by legislators, usually by private interest groups or individuals, in this case, urban working-class white men. Lobbying took many forms, including meeting lawmakers, writing letters, and organizing grassroots campaigns. Lobbying efforts were an effective way to bring attention to issues and advocate for change. Critics of lobbying today argue that it gives an unfair advantage to groups with the resources. Those who launch effective lobbying campaigns are likely to influence our legislators.

Protesting was another way urban working-class white men advocated for change. Protests took many forms, including demonstrations, marches, and sit-ins. Protests, too, were an effective way to draw attention to issues and mobilize support for a cause, but they were also disruptive and sometimes led to violence. Some people viewed protesting as a necessary form of civil disobedience, while others saw it as threatening public order.

Civil disobedience was generally intentionally disobeying laws or regulations to protest or bring about change. Civil disobedience included participating in strikes, boycotts, sit-ins, and refusing to follow the rules or policies perceived as unjust. Acts of Civil disobedience in the U.S. has a long history and have been used to bring about significant social and political change. Still, it was also controversial and sometimes led to punishment or prosecution. These forms of activism effectively drew attention to issues and influenced decision-makers, but they were also often violent, controversial, and divisive.

Populists, Women's Rights, and Suffrage

A pivotal moment in the push for expanded voting rights came in the late 19th century when the Populist Party emerged as a significant force in American politics. The Populists were a diverse group that included farmers, laborers, and urban working-class white men. They campaigned on a platform of economic and political reform, including expanding voting rights. While the Populists ultimately failed to achieve many of their goals, their efforts helped to lay the groundwork for future progress.

The 19th-century Populist Party played a significant role in expanding voting rights to urban working-class white men in the

United States, which was a considerable achievement. By challenging the restrictive system of property-based voting, the Populists helped to ensure that, eventually, all adult citizens would have a voice in their government and could shape policies that impacted their lives.

Another significant development was the rise of the women's suffrage movement, which advocated for the right of women to vote. This movement played a crucial role in challenging the notion that only men should be able to participate in the political process. Many urban working-class men supported the women's suffrage movement and helped to pass the 19th Amendment in 1920, which granted women the right to vote.

Women's suffrage was a political movement that advocated for the right of women to vote. The campaign had its roots in the early 19th century but gained significant momentum in the late 19th and early 20th centuries.

One of the principal founders of the women's suffrage movement was Susan B. Anthony, a prominent abolitionist, and women's rights activist. Anthony was arrested and fined for voting in the 1872 presidential election, and she spent the rest of her life campaigning for women's suffrage. Other important figures in the movement included Elizabeth Cady Stanton, who organized the first women's rights convention in Seneca Falls, New York, in 1848. Another important figure was Alice Paul, who led the National Women's Party and organized protests and civil disobedience campaigns to advocate for women's suffrage.

The women's suffrage movement faced significant resistance and opposition. It took many years and a great deal of organizing and advocacy to pass the 19th Amendment in 1920. This amendment was a substantial victory for the suffrage movement.

While the passage of the 19th was a significant step forward for gender equality, genuine equality for women in U.S. society remains a struggle even today. The fight for women's rights didn't end with the ratification of the 19th Amendment. Many women and men continue to work today toward full gender equality and eliminating discrimination and oppression.

There are many reasons why the struggle for women's rights continues to this day. One of the main ones is that women continue to face discrimination and inequality in many areas of daily life, including the workplace, education, and the criminal justice system.

For example, women are often paid less than men for performing the same job and are underrepresented in leadership positions in many industries. Additionally, women are often subject to harassment and assault, and they're disproportionately affected by issues such as reproductive rights and healthcare access.

Another reason the struggle for women's rights continues is that many people, both women and men, believe that gender equality is a fundamental "natural" human right. The U.S. should formally establish gender equality in the U.S. Constitution by treating all individuals fairly regardless of gender. This belief is grounded in the principle of equality, which is a core value of many democratic societies. Many people also believe that gender equality is necessary for the well-being and prosperity of the community, as it allows for all members' full participation and contribution.

Gender Equality and the ERA

The Equal Rights Amendment (ERA) is a proposed amendment to the United States Constitution that would guarantee equality under the law for all citizens, regardless of sex. The ERA was first presented in 1923 and reintroduced in every Congressional session until Congress finally passed it in 1972. Up to this point, the ratification of the ERA has not occurred. The U.S. should ensure gender equality is written in the U.S. Constitution, treating all individuals equitably without considering their gender.

Several factors currently prevent the ratification of the ERA (Equal Rights Amendment). One of the main ones is that it's faced strong opposition from some groups who argue that it could have unintended consequences, such as undermining traditional gender roles or increasing abortion rights. Some have proposed extending the ratification deadline for the ERA (Equal Rights Amendment) past the original date of 1982 while debating the process of passing it. Many people continue to strive for complete gender despite the ERA (Equal Rights Amendment) not being ratified. There are many reasons why people believe that the ERA is necessary. On March 17th, 2021, the U.S. House of Representatives finally passed a joint resolution eliminating the deadline for ratifying the Equal Rights Amendment.

As mentioned earlier, women are often paid less than men for performing the same job and are underrepresented in leadership positions in many industries. And as pointed out before, women are often subject to criminal harassment and assault, plus they're disproportionately affected by issues such as reproductive rights and healthcare access. Passage of the ERA would serve to relieve much of this discrimination.

Individuals can take various actions toward achieving gender equality, and eradicating discrimination and oppression, even if the ERA (Equal Rights Amendment) is never ratified. This work can include advocating for policy changes, supporting organizations that work toward gender equality, and engaging in grassroots activism. As individuals, we can also challenge stereotypes and biases and work to create a more inclusive and equitable society.

The ERA was proposed to guarantee equality under the law for all citizens, regardless of sex. Although not yet ratified, many individuals strive to promote gender equality and eliminate discrimination and oppression in the U.S. Meanwhile, the Equal Protection Clause of the 14th Amendment already prohibits states from denying any person within their jurisdiction " equal protection of the laws." This clause ensures that all individuals, regardless of race, ethnicity, or other characteristics, are treated equally under the law.

Regarding gender equality, the Equal Protection Clause has been used to challenge laws and practices that discriminate based on sex. For instance, individuals have used the clause to challenge laws that denied women the right to vote and laws that provided different benefits or privileges to men and women.

One notable example of the Equal Protection Clause used to challenge gender discrimination is the Supreme Court case of Reed v.

Reed (1971). In this case, the Court struck down an Idaho law that automatically preferred men over women as the administrators of estates. The Court held that the law violated the Equal Protection Clause because it treated men and women differently without a legitimate reason for doing so.

Another example is the Supreme Court case of United States v. Virginia (1996). The Court held that the Virginia Military Institute's policy of excluding women from its all-male program violated the Equal Protection Clause. The Court found that the policy wasn't substantially related to a significant governmental interest and constituted unlawful discrimination based on sex.

Another example is the Supreme Court case of Rostker v. Goldberg (1981), in which the Court upheld the constitutionality of the Military Selective Service Act, which required only men to register for the draft. The Court found the Act substantially related to a vital governmental interest (maintaining an adequate military) and therefore did not violate the Equal Protection Clause.

The Equal Protection Clause has played a crucial role in protecting individual rights and promoting equality under the law. Individuals use it to challenge discrimination against men and women and to guarantee that all individuals are treated equitably according to the Constitution. This usage includes challenging laws and practices that provide different benefits or privileges to men and women or treat them differently without a legitimate reason. The Equal Protection Clause has been an essential tool in the fight for gender equality and the protection of the rights of all individuals

The struggle for women's rights certainly didn't end with the passage of the 19th Amendment. Gender equality is not only a fundamental human right, but it's necessary for the well-being and prosperity of society. Many people are finding ways to achieve true gender equality, including advocating for policy changes, supporting organizations that work toward gender equality, and engaging in grassroots activism.

In addition to advocating for women's suffrage, to achieve their goals, the Populists worked to build alliances with other reform-minded groups, such as the women's suffrage movement and the labor movement. Through these efforts, the Populists created a broad support base and pressured lawmakers to enact change.

The Populist movement built a broad support base by organizing and mobilizing farmers, laborers, and other working people facing economic challenges and political disenfranchisement. Through tactics such as strikes, protests, and political organizing, the Populists were able to put pressure on lawmakers to enact change and address the issues that mattered to their supporters. The Populists successfully advocated for policies such as the free coinage of silver, which would have benefited farmers and other debtors, and in bringing attention to the need for broader economic and political reforms.

Adopting the Australian Ballot

A turning point in the Populist push for expanded voting rights came in the early 1890s when they successfully lobbied for the passage of the Australian ballot. By enforcing the Australian method of secret ballots in U.S. elections, this reform aimed to prevent voter intimidation and ensure that all citizens could vote without fear of repercussions. The Australian ballot was a significant victory for the Populists and helped pave the way for further voting reforms.

Before adopting the Australian ballot, corrupt practices and intimidation were standard during elections in the United States. The adoption of the Australian ballot helped to mitigate these issues. Political Parties and employers repeatedly pressured or coerced voters to support particular candidates, and there was little privacy or secrecy in the voting process.

The Australian ballot changed this by introducing a system in which voters marked their votes privately. The polls were then counted in a centralized location, away from the influence of political parties and employers.

Adopting the Australian ballot was a significant victory for voting reform, as it helped to level the playing field and give working-class voters more control over the electoral process. It also paved the way for further voting reforms, such as adopting universal suffrage and eliminating poll taxes and other barriers to voting.

Poll taxes were a common form of voter suppression in the United States, particularly in the South. These taxes required people to pay a fee to vote and were often used to disenfranchise poor and minority voters. The Populists worked to eliminate poll taxes and other barriers to voting, arguing that they were unfair and violated the principle of universal suffrage.

In addition to poll taxes, the Populists also worked to eliminate other barriers to voting, such as literacy tests and discriminatory registration practices. These practices disenfranchised minority and low-income voters disproportionately, and the Populists believed they were unjust and violated the right to vote.

Populist efforts to expand voting rights and eliminate barriers to voting were ultimately successful. They helped pave the way for greater democracy and political participation in the United States. The Populists' efforts were also essential to the civil rights and equality struggle.

The adoption of the Australian ballot was among the most significant steps forward in the struggle for democracy and fair elections in the U.S. It helped to empower working-class Americans and to give them a stronger voice in the political process. It also set the stage for further voting reforms that continue to shape how we participate in elections today.

The Populists were unable to accomplish many of their goals. Other reform movements eventually overtook them, as the Populists couldn't establish a strong presence in national politics. However, their legacy lived on, and their efforts helped to lay the groundwork for future progress in voting reform.

The Populist push for expanded voting rights contributed to a more inclusive and democratic political process, and their contributions have had a lasting impact. In the end, the efforts of urban working-class white men to expand their voting rights were successful, although it took many years and a great deal of struggle.

Their contributions have had a lasting impact on American society and continue to shape our political landscape.

Through Populist reforms, by the end of the 1820s, attitudes and State laws had changed in favor of universal white male suffrage. All white men would soon vote. Urban working-class white men would have their voices heard for the first time. The 1828 election of President Andrew Jackson was the first in which non-property-holding white males could vote in most U.S. States.

The Campaign of 1828

The campaign of 1828 was a pivotal event in developing a two-party system in the U.S. The campaign significantly changed the conduct of presidential elections and the executive branch's power. Intense political polarization and personal attacks characterized the election campaign. 1828 marked the end of the so-called "Era of Good Feelings," a period of relative political harmony in the United States.

Among the factors that contributed to the shift in the 1828 presidential campaign was the emergence of political Parties. Before this campaign, presidential elections had been largely nonpartisan affairs, with candidates running as independents and focusing on their qualifications and experience rather than their Party affiliations. However, in the 1828 campaign, the Democratic-Republican Party, led by Andrew Jackson, and the National Republican Party, led by John Quincy Adams, emerged as major political Parties, engaging in intense campaigning and advertising. These party establishments marked the beginning of the modern two-party system in the United States.

The 1828 campaign was also notable for the emergence of a new form of political campaigning. The campaign of 1828 used slogans and symbols. It also introduced the distribution of campaign literature. Mass rallies and everyday public speaking marked the campaign. These are significantly more prevalent in today's political campaigns, especially among extremist partisans than in 1828. These tactics helped mobilize voters, increase public interest in the campaign, and set the stage for the modern political campaign process.

The 1828 campaign marked a significant transformation in the conduct of presidential elections and the executive branch's power. It marked the emergence of political Parties and modern campaign tactics. It also set the stage for the extent of political polarization and campaigning that have again characterized presidential elections in the United States since the Richard M. Nixon administration ended in August 1974.

A significant contributing factor to this polarizing shift was the increasing importance of political Parties in the early 19th century. Before the campaign of 1828, political Parties were relatively weak, and candidates were largely independent.

However, as the campaign of 1828 approached, the Democratic-Republican Party and the National Republican Party emerged as the two dominant Parties in the U.S. These Parties began engaging in more organized and structured campaigning. They started to develop platforms and policies that differentiated them from one another.

Another factor that contributed to the shift in the campaign of 1828 was the increasing use of electioneering tactics that bore a closer resemblance to modern political campaigning. Electioneering included the use of Party conventions, campaign slogans, and political rallies. Candidates also began to rely more on the media, including newspapers and other print media, to get their message out to the public.

The campaign of 1828 was also significant because it marked a strengthening of the executive branch's power. Before this campaign, the presidency was a relatively weak office with little absolute authority. However, as the election of 1828 approached, the candidates began to present themselves as leaders who could take bold action and make real change. This presentation helped elevate the presidency to a more prominent position in American politics and increased the public's expectations of what the U.S. president could do. This election campaign was a pivotal event that marked a turning point in the conduct of presidential elections, strengthening the executive branch's power and laying the foundation of the current political landscape.

The 15th Amendment and Voter Discrimination

It's important to note that African-American men, and other men of color, were denied the right to vote in the United States for much of the country's history due to various discriminatory laws and practices. State and local governments implemented laws that explicitly barred African-American men and other men of color from voting. Individuals and state authorities used voter intimidation, poll taxes, and literacy tests to discourage or prevent men of color from participating in the political process.

Individuals and state authorities in the United States used intimidation, taxes, and literacy tests to discourage or prevent these men from participating in the political process, even after ratifying the 15th Amendment. Adopted in 1870, the 15th granted all men of color, including African-American men, the right to vote. It states, "The right of citizens of the United States to vote shall not be denied or abridged by the United States or by any State on account of race, color, or previous condition of servitude." Despite this constitutional amendment, many States used various tactics to effectively deny African-American men and other men of color the right to vote.

Violence and intimidation at polling places were primarily used to intimidate these voters. These tactics could be physical threats, violence against voters, or the presence of white mobs at polling places as intimidation. In some instances, individuals or groups killed voters of color for attempting to exercise their right to vote.

Another tactic used to discourage African-American voting was the implementation of voting taxation. Poll taxes were fees that voters had to pay to vote, disproportionately affecting poor African-American voters who may not have had the financial resources to pay them. In addition, many States required that poll taxes be paid in advance, which made it even more difficult for poor African-American voters to participate in elections.

Finally, literacy tests were another tactic used to discourage African-American voting. Individuals or groups used tests to determine whether an individual was literate and to disqualify voters. Individuals or groups administering these tests in a discriminatory way often provided more accessible tests to white voters or passed them even if they failed. They essentially denied the right to vote to many African-Americans and voters of color by their inability to pass these tests.

The single most significant factor contributing to the denial of voting rights to African-American men was the legacy of slavery in the United States. Before the Civil War, African-American men weren't considered citizens and weren't afforded the same rights and protections as white men. Characterization as noncitizens meant they were excluded from the political process and had no say in the decisions that impacted their lives.

A succeeding factor contributing to the denial of voting rights to these men was the rise of segregation and Jim Crow laws in the post-Civil War period. These laws created a system of racial segregation and discrimination that further marginalized African-American men, making it very difficult for them to participate in the political process.

The Jim Crow laws were a set of State and local laws that enforced racial segregation and discrimination specifically against African-American people, particularly African-American men, from the late 19th century to the mid-20th century. Jim Crow laws, primarily in the Southern States, were named after a minstrel show character that a white actor portrayed in blackface.

The Jim Crow laws marginalized African-American men in many ways, making it difficult for them to participate in the nation's political process, among many other discriminatory practices. The most significant way these laws marginalized them was by denying them the right to vote.

Many Southern States implemented voting restrictions such as the formerly mentioned literacy tests and poll taxes, which disproportionately affected African-American voters, effectively denying them the vote. In addition, these voters were often subjected to intimidation and violence at polling places, further discouraging them from participating in elections.

Significantly, Jim Crow laws also limited the economic opportunities available to African-American men. These laws enforced segregation in various settings, including schools, public accommodations, and workplaces. Segregation effectively limited the ability of people of color to access specific jobs and career paths and receive an education that was on par with their white counterparts.

In addition to the economic and political limitations, Jim Crow laws imposed social and cultural restrictions on people of color. These laws enforced segregation in social settings, such as restaurants, theaters, and other places of entertainment. They also imposed strict codes of behavior.

The U.S. Constitution was amended with the 15th Amendment in 1870, granting African-American men and men of color the right to vote. This change started to change the situation over time. Ratification was a significant milestone in the struggle for civil rights and marked the beginning of a new era in American politics. However, despite this progress, African-American men faced significant voting barriers.

The Voting Rights Act of 1965 formally dismantled the barriers preventing African-Americans from exercising their right to vote and fully franchised them. This landmark legislation prohibited States from using literacy tests or other discriminatory practices to deny voting rights to citizens. It also established federal oversight of elections to ensure all citizens have an equal opportunity to participate in the political process.

One of the earliest efforts to expand the right to vote for women in the United States was the Seneca Falls Convention of 1848, where a group of women's rights activists, including Elizabeth Cady Stanton and Lucretia Mott, gathered to discuss the rights and status of women in society. At this convention, attendees adopted the "Declaration of Sentiments," outlining how women were denied equal rights, and called for the expansion of the right to vote for women.

Despite these early efforts, it would take more than 70 years before women could vote nationally. The 19th Amendment to the United States Constitution, ratified in 1920, finally granted women the right to vote. This amendment, too, marked a significant milestone in the struggle for voting rights and helped to bring about a more equal and democratic society. The 19th Amendment and the Voting Rights Act of 1965 also helped ensure that women of color could exercise their franchise, which they had often been denied.

Minority Citizenship and the Vote

Native Americans, also known as "American Indians," have had a complex and often tumultuous history with the United States government. Despite being the original inhabitants of the land now known as the United States, Native Americans weren't granted citizenship until 1924, more than 148 years after the country's founding.

Before the Indian Citizenship Act of 1924, Native Americans were "wards of the State," a designation that denied them many rights and protections afforded to other citizens. The U.S. Government granted Native Americans citizenship by passing the Indian Citizenship Act of 1924, which changed their legal status. Before that time, the government forced Native Americans to live on reservations and denied them rights such as voting, owning land, or even leaving these reservations without permission.

The push for Native American citizenship began in the late 19th century when several Native American leaders began advocating for the rights and freedoms of their people. Chief Standing Bear of the Ponca Tribe challenged how the U.S. government treated his tribe. He is widely recognized as one of the first Native American leaders to do so.

In 1879, Chief Standing Bear sued the government to have his tribe recognized as a sovereign nation with the right to self-governance and the protection of their land and resources. It took another 45 years for Native Americans to be granted citizenship, despite efforts to achieve that.

In 1924, the Indian Citizenship Act was passed, granting citizenship to all Native Americans born in the United States. This act also allowed Native Americans to vote, though many States continued to impose voting restrictions on them, such as literacy tests and other discriminatory measures.

The Voting Rights Act of 1965 granted Native Americans, among other marginalized groups such as African-Americans, full voting rights. The Act made it illegal for States to impose voting restrictions based on race, and it helped to ensure that all citizens, including Native Americans, had equal access to the ballot box.

Today, Native Americans continue to face many challenges, including high rates of poverty, poor access to healthcare, and ongoing struggles with issues of sovereignty and self-determination. However, the right to vote and the recognition of their citizenship have been essential steps toward justice and equality for Native Americans.

It's important to note that contrary to urban myths, denying Jews and citizens of other religions the right to vote in the United States was never a formal policy or law. However, throughout history, various laws and practices effectively denied Jews and other minority groups the right to vote, such as the poll tax, literacy tests, and other voting restrictions that disproportionately affected their minority communities. These practices were often motivated by prejudice and discrimination and were used to maintain the political power of the majority group.

One example of a law that may have effectively denied Jews the right to vote was the Alien and Sedition Acts of 1798. These Acts were passed during political tension between the United States and France. These Acts made it more difficult for immigrants, including Jews, to become naturalized citizens and thus gain the right to vote. The Acts also criminalized certain types of speech critical of the government, which could have chilled the political participation of Jews and other minority groups.

1798 Alien and Sedition Acts

The Alien and Sedition Acts of 1798 were four laws passed by the United States Congress during significant political tensions between the U.S. and France. The first of the Alien and Sedition Acts, the Naturalization Act, increased the time required for immigrants to become naturalized citizens from five to fourteen years. This time limitation made it more difficult for immigrants, including Jews, to gain the right to vote and participate in politics.

The second Act, the Alien Friends Act, gave the President the authority to deport any non-citizen deemed "dangerous to the peace and safety of the United States." This Act targeted immigrants, particularly those from France, and may have been used to target Jews and other minority groups.

The third Act, the Alien Enemies Act, allowed the President to deport male citizens of countries where the United States was at war, again targeting immigrants and potentially including Jews.

The fourth and final Act, the Sedition Act, criminalized speech or writing critical of the government, the President, or Congress. This Act chilled political participation, as individuals who were critical of the government could be punished for expressing their views. This criminalization could have negatively impacted minority groups, including Jews, who may have been more hesitant to speak out against the government for fear of reprisal.

While the Alien and Sedition Acts of 1798 made it more difficult for immigrants, including Jews, to become naturalized citizens and gain the right to vote, several reasons led to repeal. One reason was that they were widely unpopular at their passage and in the years following. Many Americans saw these acts as an attempt by the Federalist Party, which was in power then, to suppress dissent and silence its political opponents. This unpopularity led to significant opposition to the acts within Congress and among the general public.

Another reason for abolishing the Alien and Sedition Acts was that they were considered unconstitutional. Many Americans believed these acts violated the 1st Amendment's protection of freedom of speech and the press. The Supreme Court later upheld this belief in cases such as New York Times Co. v. Sullivan and Tinker v. Des Moines Independent Community School District.

United States political climate changed, leading to the abolition of the Alien and Sedition Acts. By the early 19th century, the Federalist Party had lost power. The Democratic-Republican Party, which opposed the acts, had come to dominate American politics, and the Acts were allowed to expire.

Over time, however, there have been significant changes to laws and practices that have ensured naturalized immigrants, Jews, and other religious minority citizen groups have the right to vote in the United States. Again, the most significant of these changes was the adoption of the 15th Amendment to the United States Constitution in 1870, prohibiting the denial of the right to vote based on race, color, or previous condition of servitude. This amendment which, again, was part of the Reconstruction Amendments passed after the Civil War, helped to ensure that African-Americans, other men of color, and many Jews, were able to vote.

Other critical legislative actions expanded the right to vote for Jews and other groups, including the 19th Amendment, which granted women the right to vote in 1920, and the Voting Rights Act of 1965, which prohibited racial discrimination in voting and established federal oversight of elections in areas with a history of discrimination. These laws and others promoting voting rights have helped create a more inclusive and democratic society in the United States.

Throughout history, laws and practices may have denied Jews and other religious groups the right to vote in the United States. Changes, including the 15th, 19th, and Voting Rights Acts, have helped promote a more inclusive and just society in the United States, but much work remains. These laws have contributed to the ongoing effort to protect and expand the right to vote for all Americans.

Chapter 3

Let's Have a Party

Political Parties have played a significant role in the development of modern democracy. Great Britain in the late 17th and early 18th centuries gave birth to the first political parties in world history. Early Parties, like the Tories and the Whigs, were formed in response to the Glorious Revolution of 1688 and Britain's subsequent establishment of a constitutional monarchy.

The Glorious Revolution of 1688 in England resulted in the deposition of King James II and the accession of his daughter Mary and her husband William of Orange to the throne. James II sparked the revolution by attempting to assert his authority over the English Parliament and promoting Catholicism. The Glorious Revolution comprised a broad coalition of politicians and citizens, including Tories and Whigs. The revolution resulted in the English political system becoming more parliamentary. The events of the Glorious Revolution also led to the development of the modern concept of political Parties, with the Tories and Whigs being England's first central political Parties.

Political Parties emerged as a way for people with shared political beliefs to organize and advocate for their views. A single leader or a small group of influential individuals created early political parties, often based on personal and family connections.

The Democratic-Republican Party is Born

The United States has a long and complex political history. The establishment of the first two major political Parties, the Democratic-Republican Party and the National-Republican Party played a significant role in shaping the early political landscape of the country.

The Democratic-Republican Party, founded in 1792 by Thomas Jefferson and James Madison, was the first organized political Party in the United States. This Party was based on the principles of democracy and republicanism and sought to limit the federal government's power and protect states' and individuals' rights.

One of the fundamental principles of the Democratic-Republican Party was democracy. The Party believed in the principle of majority rule and supported the expansion of suffrage to include more people, including white men who didn't own property. The Party also supported the idea of a federal government more responsive to the people's will and less beholden to the wealthy and powerful.

A significant component of the Democratic-Republican Party's political philosophy was republicanism. They believed in the principles of limited government and the protection of individual rights. This belief meant the Party sought to determine the federal government's power and protect the sovereignty of the States. They also believed in the right to own property and free speech.

In terms of how the Democratic-Republican Party sought to limit the power of the federal government, they supported the idea of a federal government that was more decentralized and less powerful. This party was formed believing that the federal government's powers should be limited and the States should have more autonomy in governing themselves. This political philosophy reflected a belief in support of a weaker central government with a more vital role for the States.

The Democratic-Republican Party also sought to protect States and individual rights through its commitment to federalism. Their Party believed the federal government should have a limited role in the affairs of the States and that the States should be free to govern themselves as they saw fit. The Party supported States' rights and protected individual liberty. Their Party platform had emerged in response to the Federalist Party, which was too centralized and supportive of a large national government, paid for at the expense of the States. The Federalist Party was active in the U.S. during the late 18th and early 19th centuries.

Founded by Alexander Hamilton, John Adams, and other supporters of a strong national government, the Federalists opposed the Democratic-Republican Party, which advocated for a decentralized government and the protection of States' rights. Instead, the Federalists supported a strong central government, a national bank, and a strong military.

The Federalists were generally more favorable to business and commerce than the Democratic-Republicans. The Federalist Party was also the dominant political Party in the United States during the presidency of John Adams. Still, it began to decline in power following the election of Thomas Jefferson in 1800. Eventually, the Federalist Party faded from national prominence and dissolved by the end of the 1820s.

Yet, many Democratic-Republicans also emerged from the Federalists. The Federalist Party reflected its core belief by supporting a national bank, strengthening the federal government's financial power. They persistently argued that protecting States' and individuals' rights was critically necessary to help ensure power wouldn't be concentrated in a single, centralized entity.

To further this goal, the Democratic-Republicans began to support a stricter interpretation of the Constitution, which they believed would ensure the national government wouldn't exceed its delegated powers. States would retain a significant degree of autonomy through this more stringent interpretation. They also advocated for a Bill of Rights to safeguard the rights and freedoms of individuals against potential abuses of government power.

The commitment of the Democratic-Republican Party to the protection of States' rights and individual liberties had a significant impact on the continuing development of the United States as a nation.

It also helped shape the power balance between the national government and the States while safeguarding the rights of individuals against potential abuses of government power. This commitment to protecting States' rights and individual liberties remains a core tenet of the modern Democratic Party.

Today's Democratic Party was founded on the principles of democracy and republicanism. These principles are more responsive to the people's will and less beholden to the interests of the wealthy and powerful while protecting individual liberty and the autonomy of the States.

National-Republican Party and Federalism

The National-Republican Party was also known as the Federalist Party. It was founded in 1792 by Alexander Hamilton and other supporters of a strong central government. The Party favored a strong centralized federal government and a national bank. It also supported a more centralized economy with government oversight.

The National-Republican Party was committed to a large federal government, a national bank, and a vastly more centralized government. The Party believed the federal government should have an active role in most of the nation's affairs and should be able to exert its power and influence more decisively. This Party believed a national bank would benefit the country by providing a stable source of credit and greater financial stability. They also thought that a national bank would help to create a more centralized form of government, serving as a central hub for the nation's financial affairs.

The National-Republican Party also favored a powerful federal government that could exert its influence over the States. The Party believed a centralized government would address the nation's needs more efficiently and effectively.

Both political Parties engaged in organized and structured campaigning, using newspapers, pamphlets, and other forms of the era's media to promote their candidates and policies. They also held conventions to nominate candidates for office and to adopt Party platforms.

The main difference between the two Parties was their views about the extent of the federal government's role. The Democratic-Republicans believed in a limited federal government and strong States' rights, while the National-Republicans favored a stronger central government and a more centralized economy.

The Parties also had different policies on various issues, including taxation, trade, and foreign affairs. The Democratic-Republicans were generally more protective of States' rights and individual freedoms, while the National-Republicans favored a more interventionist government and a strong national defense.

The Democratic-Republican Party and the National-Republican Party each played significant roles in shaping the early political landscape of the United States. Their differences in policies and platforms continue to influence American politics.

It's important to note that the Democratic-Republican Party eventually split into the Democratic Party and the Republican Party. One of the main reasons for the split of the Democratic-Republican Party was the issue of slavery.

Divisions emerged within the Party over whether to allow slavery to expand into new territories. Those who supported slavery, known as the "slave power," believed it was necessary for the economy and argued that the Constitution protected it. Those who opposed slavery, known as the "free soilers," thought it was morally wrong and argued that it should be contained and eventually abolished.

As the issue of slavery became more divisive, the Democratic-Republican Party began to fracture. In 1828, Andrew Jackson, a slaveholding Democrat from Tennessee, was elected President. In addition to ushering in a new, more powerful role for the U.S. Presidency, Andrew Jackson represented a new direction for the Party as both a nationalist and a populist.

Many issues, including slavery, tariffs, and States' rights, caused division between the two parties. These actions contributed to the growing rift within the Democratic-Republican Party. Jackson's aggressive style and tendency to rely on his judgment rather than seeking the advice of Congress were also contributing factors. This behavior may sound familiar to the reader, as a later U.S. President, Donald J. Trump, who has been identified as both a nationalist and populist, also modeled his presidency on Andrew Jackson's.

Jackson's aggressive style and tendency to rely on his judgment rather than seeking the advice of Congress contributed to the growing rift within the Democratic-Republican Party. Many Northern Democrats began to defect to the newly formed Republican Party, founded in the mid-1850s. This new Party was opposed to the expansion of slavery. The Republican Party, supported by many abolitionists and other opponents of slavery, eventually overtook the Democratic-Republican Party as the dominant political Party in the North and played a significant role in the eventual abolition of slavery in the United States.

Andrew Jackson's presidency marked a significant shift in the direction of the Democratic-Republican Party. His election contributed to the emergence of the Republican Party as a powerful political force in the United States.

By the 1850s, the Democratic Party had become the dominant Party in the South, while the Republican Party had become the dominant Party in the North. Many issues, including slavery, tariffs, and States' rights, divided the two Parties. The split between the two became more pronounced during the Civil War, as the Democrats supported the Confederacy, and the Republicans supported the Union.

The issue of slavery primarily caused the split between the Democratic Party and the Republican Party, as it was at the heart of their conflict. The Democrats, primarily in the South, supported both the institution and enterprise of slavery, believing that the Constitution protected it. During the Civil War, the Republicans, the dominant Party in the North, considered slavery a moral wrong that should be abolished, so they vehemently opposed it. Many American lives were lost during the Civil War due to this moral conflict.

States' Rights Versus Centralized Fed

Another reason for the deepening split between the Democrats and the Republicans during the Civil War was the issue of States' rights. The Democrats supported the idea of States' rights, believing States should have more autonomy in governing themselves. The Party based its position on a longstanding commitment to federalism and the belief that the States were sovereign entities with the right to make their own decisions. An example of how the Democrats supported States' rights during the Civil War was their opposition to the Union's use of federal power to suppress the Confederacy. The Democrats argued that the Union had no right to use military force to impose its will on the Southern States and that the States had the right to secede if they chose to do so.

Another example of the Democrats' support for States' rights was their opposition to the Reconstruction policies implemented by the Republican-controlled Congress after the war. The Democrats argued that these policies infringed on the Southern states' sovereignty and that they should be allowed to govern themselves without federal interference.

The Democrats' support for States' rights during the Civil War was motivated by their belief in a decentralized government. They adopted a position of protecting the rights of both States and individuals and believed in preventing the concentration of power into a single centralized entity.

Abraham Lincoln led Republicans to argue that the Union should be preserved at all costs and for a strong federal government to achieve this end. Lincoln viewed the preservation of the Union as crucial to the survival of the United States as a nation. He was willing to use the federal government's power to achieve this goal.

The Republican Party's belief in nationalism and the United States as a single, indivisible nation formed the basis for their position. One example of the Republicans' belief in a stronger federal government was their support for the Union's use of military force to suppress the Confederacy. The Republicans argued that the Union had a duty to preserve the nation's integrity and that military force was necessary to achieve this goal.

Another example of the Republicans' support for a strong federal government was their implementation of Reconstruction policies after the Civil war. The federal government designed these policies to rebuild the southern States and ensure their full integration into the Union. The Republicans argued their policies would ensure the stability and unity of the nation after the war and that the federal government had a responsibility to enforce them.

Republican belief in a stronger federal government during the Civil War was motivated by their commitment to nationalism and the preservation of the Union. They believed that they must preserve the Union of States at all costs.

A third reason for the deepening split between the Democrats and the Republicans during the Civil War was the issue of tariffs. The Democrats opposed high tariffs, which they saw as a burden on Southern farmers, while the Republicans supported high taxes to protect Northern industry.

Before the Civil War, the Democrats had vehemently opposed higher tariffs, which they saw as an undue burden on Southern farmers. The Democrats labeled these taxes "protectionist," imposed to safeguard Northern industry while undermining Southern agriculture. The Democrats argued these tariffs caused financial harm to the southern states. They also believed these tariffs disproportionately affected the economy of the southern states, creating a regional economic inequity.

Compromises and Acts of Civil War

Another example of the Democrats' opposition to high tariffs was their support for the Compromise of 1850, which included a tax reduction. Democrats believed this compromise would help to ease growing tensions between the North and South and prevent the outbreak of war.

The Compromise of 1850 was a package of five bills passed by the United States Congress to address the issue of slavery and ease tensions between the North and South. Senator Henry Clay proposed the compromise, and President Millard Fillmore supported it.

One of the provisions of the Compromise of 1850 was the Fugitive Slave Act, which required individuals to assist in capturing and returning runaway slaves. The Act imposed heavy fines and prison sentences on those who assisted in their escape. Abolitionists and others who opposed slavery also opposed this provision. People also viewed it as an attempt to spread slavery into the North.

The Compromise of 1850 was the admission of California as a free State, which helped to balance the number of free and slave States in the Union. The North rejected the Compromise of 1850 because they believed it did not sufficiently address the issue of slavery and instead sought to preserve the status quo. California's admission only stirred more controversy in the nation about slavery.

The North rejected the Compromise of 1850, as they believed it did not adequately address the issue of slavery. They sought to preserve the status quo. The compromise was a temporary solution that did little to address the underlying tensions between the North and South. More importantly, it ultimately contributed to the outbreak of the Civil War.

Yet another example of the Democrats' opposition to high tariffs was their support for the Kansas-Nebraska Act of 1854. This Act was controversial legislation that allowed for extending slavery into new territories in the western United States. Democrats supported the Compromise of 1850 because they believed it would help balance the interests of the North and South, reduce the burden of high tariffs on Southern farmers, and reduce tensions between the two regions.

One of the ways the Democrats supported the Kansas-Nebraska Act of 1854 was the Party's commitment to popular sovereignty, which allowed the residents of a territory to determine whether it would be a free or slave State. The Democrats believed this approach would allow for a peaceful resolution to the issue of slavery and prevent the outbreak of war.

Another example of their support for the Act was the Party's belief it would help to preserve the balance of power between the North and South. The Democrats argued that the act would ensure the North and South had equal representation in Congress and prevent the North from gaining an unfair advantage over the South.

The Kansas-Nebraska Act of 1854s was controversial legislation that led to the expansion of slavery into the territories of Kansas and Nebraska. Many pro-slavery Democrats at the time opposed the act primarily because it threatened the stability of the Union. Abolitionists and others who opposed slavery caused the most opposition to the Act. The intense abolitionist opposition widened the divide between the North and South, leading to the Civil War.

Republicans had supported high tariffs as a way to protect Northern industry. They'd argued these tariffs would help to create a level playing field for American manufacturers. The Republicans also believed that higher taxes would generate more revenue for the federal government, which they would use to fund public works projects and other initiatives.

The Republicans argued these tariffs would protect American businesses from foreign competition, creating new job opportunities and stimulating economic growth. They believed this would help make for a more competitive market for American companies and ensure they could thrive.

The political split between the Democratic and Republican Parties became even more pronounced during the Civil War due to the issues of slavery, States' rights, and tariffs. Democrats supported the Confederacy and the institution of slavery, while the Republicans supported the Union and the abolition of slavery. The two Parties had deep divisions over these issues. The conflict of the Civil War exacerbated their divisions and further entrenched the split between them.

Interestingly, the Democratic Party, founded in 1828, is the oldest surviving political Party in the United States and is still active today. Although the Republican Party often refers to itself as the GOP or "Grand Old Party," it was founded in 1854, 26 years later than the Democratic Party. The Republican Party is also active today and is one of the two major political Parties in the United States.

It's also interesting to note how much the GOP, or Republican Party, has evolved and its principles have changed since the Civil War. Republicans have remained committed to limited government, individual freedom, and personal responsibility. The GOP has traditionally supported a strong national defense and free trade. In recent years though, the Republican Party has also come to be associated with social conservatism, including opposition to abortion and same-sex marriage. This association with social conservatism has evolved, and several factors have contributed to it.

The Republican Party has typically been known for supporting financial conservatism; however, in recent years, it has also gained a reputation for its adherence to social conservatism, including its opposition to abortion and same-sex marriage. Over time, various factors have influenced the party to shift its stance.

One major factor is the role of religious conservatives within the Party. Many religious conservatives, particularly evangelicals, have been drawn to the Republican Party due to its stance on abortion and same-sex marriage. Religious conservatives have framed these issues as moral and religious and have deemed them particularly important.

Another factor that's contributed to the association of the Republican Party with social conservatism is the Party's focus on individual freedom and limited government. Many Republicans believe that government should not be involved in issues such as abortion and same-sex marriage and that individuals and their families should make these decisions. This belief has led to the Party's opposition to abortion, same-sex marriage, and other social issues such as assisted suicide and drug legalization.

The Republican Party's base of support also influences the party. Many of the Party's supporters come from rural and suburban areas, which tend to be more socially conservative than urban areas.

As a result, the Party has had to consider these voters' views, who often prioritize social issues such as abortion and same-sex marriage.

Many factors have influenced the evolution of the Republican Party's association with social conservatism, none more so than the role of religious conservatives within the party, the party's focus on individual freedom and limited government, and the views of its base of support.

This association with the Republican "base" has had significant consequences for the Republican Party and American politics more generally. The debate over social issues has often been a critical dividing line between the two major political Parties. Highly divergent core ideologies and associated principles are the fundamental reason for staunch partisan opposition between the two major political Parties in the U. S.

Social Conservatism and Liberalism

Opposing the expansion of slavery has partly contributed to the GOP's association with social conservatism. As previously mentioned, many of the Party's founders were abolitionists and supporters of the "Free Soil" movement, which sought to keep the western territories free from slavery. This history contributed to the GOP's reputation as a Party committed to traditional values and protecting individual rights.

Another factor contributing to the GOP's association with social conservatism is its focus on limited government and individual freedom. The Party has traditionally supported a smaller, less intrusive government and has opposed government intervention in social and personal matters. This position has led the GOP to oppose policies such as abortion and same-sex marriage, which many social conservatives see as threats to traditional values and the natural order of things.

The religious beliefs of its members and supporters have also influenced the GOP's association with social conservatism. Many members of the Party are religious conservatives who believe in the importance of traditional family values and oppose policies they see as contrary to their beliefs. This conservative viewpoint has led the GOP to take extreme positions on issues such as abortion and same-sex marriage that align with the views of its religious voter base.

In summary, the GOP's association with social conservatism, including its opposition to abortion and same-sex marriage, has been influenced by several factors, including its history as a Party founded to oppose the expansion of slavery, its focus on limited government and individual freedom, and the religious beliefs of its members and supporters. These associations have played a significant role in shaping the Republican Party's political platform and have contributed to its reputation as a Party committed to traditional values and protecting individual rights.

Despite its evolution and changes in focus, the GOP, or Republican Party, has remained a major political force in the United States and has played a significant role in shaping the country's political landscape. The Republicans produced many notable leaders, including Abraham Lincoln, Theodore Roosevelt, and Ronald Reagan, and they've consistently been significant players in national elections.

The Democratic Party has a long history of being associated with social liberalism and greater taxation, including support for abortion and same-sex marriage. This association has evolved, and many factors have contributed to it.

One factor contributing to the Democratic Party's association with social liberalism is its history as a Party that has supported social and economic justice. From its origins as the Party of Thomas Jefferson and Andrew Jackson, the Democrats have traditionally supported policies that aim to promote equality and address social and economic inequality. This commitment has led the Party to support policies such as abortion and same-sex marriage, which Democrats believe are necessary for protecting individual rights and promoting equality.

Another factor contributing to the Democratic Party's association with social liberalism is its focus on government intervention and social welfare programs. The Party has traditionally supported a larger, more active government that addresses social and economic problems and assists those in need. This position has led the Party to support higher taxes and increased government spending, which are seen as necessary to fund these programs and address social and economic issues.

The views of its members and supporters have also influenced the Democratic Party's association with social liberalism. Many modern-day Democrats are social liberals believing in the importance of individual freedom and the protection of individual rights. They support policies such as abortion and same-sex marriage as essential for promoting these values.

The Democratic Party's association with social liberalism and greater taxation, including its support for abortion and same-sex marriage, has been influenced by many factors, including its history as a Party supportive of social and economic justice, its focus on government intervention and social welfare programs, and the views of its members and supporters. These associations have played a significant role in shaping the Party's political platform and have contributed to its reputation as a Party committed to social and economic justice and protecting individual rights.

The two early-era Parties had different views on the federal government's role and policies on various issues. The Democratic-Republican Party and the National-Republican Party also differed in their demographic bases, much like the two major Parties today. Farmers and people living in rural areas primarily supported the Democratic-Republican Party, while urban dwellers and the wealthy more commonly supported the National-Republican Party.

Throughout their histories, both Parties have undergone significant changes and evolution. The Democratic Party traditionally associates with liberal and progressive policies, and the Republican Party generally associates with more conservative and libertarian policies. However, these associations have not always been consistent, and both Parties have had factions and divisions within their ranks.

Despite their differences, both Parties have contributed to developing the United States as a democratic republic and have played a vital role in its political system. Having two political parties allows for a diversity of viewpoints and ideas to be represented in the political process, and it helps to ensure that the government responds to the needs and concerns of the American people.

Political Parties continue to play a crucial role in our modern democracy. They serve as a way for people with shared political beliefs to unite and advocate for their views. Political Parties also provide a way for citizens to hold their elected representatives accountable, and they help to ensure that the government is responsive to the needs and concerns of the people. Not everyone agrees. Some argue that the practice of partisanship is a reason for the abolition of the Party system.

Political Partisanship

A troubling outgrowth of political Parties is the practice of partisanship, which refers to solid loyalty and support for a particular political Party. It's been a part of the American political landscape since the Republic's early days. As political parties emerged in the late 18th century, they represented a way for people with shared political beliefs to organize and advocate for their views. They have also played a significant role in developing the U.S. form of modern democracy.

The Democratic-Republican Party, the first organized political Party in the United States, was based on the principles of democracy and republicanism. The National-Republican Party, the Federalist Party, was founded to support a strong central government.

Over time, these early political Parties evolved and changed, and new Parties emerged to represent different viewpoints and interests. However, partisanship can also lead to political polarization and make it more difficult for politicians to work together to find common ground on important issues.

In recent years, there has been increasing concern about the impact of partisanship on the American political system. There have been efforts to promote bipartisanship and political cooperation to address this issue. Still, both Parties have practiced gaining an advantage in elections by undermining the voting rights of certain groups.

Many believe partisanship has led to increased gridlock in Congress, making it more difficult for lawmakers to work together and find common ground on important issues. In response to these concerns, efforts have been made to promote bipartisanship and political cooperation.

Bipartisanship refers to the willingness of lawmakers from different political Parties to work together to find common ground on issues. Some people believe bipartisanship is essential for the effective functioning of the political system and can help reduce polarization and gridlock. Individuals and groups have made significant efforts in recent years to promote bipartisanship by creating organizations and initiatives that bring lawmakers from different Parties together to work on common goals.

Gerrymandering, Voter IDs, Roll Purges

Despite many efforts, partisanship remains a significant factor in American politics. Both Parties have often engaged in practices that seek to gain an advantage in elections by undermining the voting rights of certain groups. For example, both Parties have been accused of gerrymandering, redrawing electoral districts to benefit one Party. Both Parties have been accused of engaging in voter suppression tactics, such as imposing strict voter ID requirements or purging voter rolls, which can make it more difficult for certain groups to vote.

Gerrymandering is about redrawing electoral districts to benefit one political Party over the other. Accusers have claimed that the Democratic and Republican Parties engage in this type of voter suppression to gain an advantage in elections.

An example of gerrymandering by the Democratic Party occurred in Maryland in 2011. Democrats in the State legislature redrew the boundaries of the State's congressional districts to concentrate Republican voters in a few communities while spreading Democratic voters out more evenly across the State. Someone implemented a redistricting plan, resulting in Democrats having a 7-1 advantage in the State's congressional delegation, even though the State's voters were evenly divided between the two Parties.

Accusers have claimed that the Republican Party engages in gerrymandering too. An example occurred in North Carolina in 2016 when the State's Republican-controlled legislature redrew the boundaries of the State's congressional districts in a way that favored Republicans. Someone implemented a redistricting plan which resulted in Republicans having a 10-3 advantage in the State's congressional delegation, again, even though the State's voters were evenly split between the two Parties.

In addition to gerrymandering, both Parties have been accused of using other voter suppression tactics, such as imposing strict voter ID requirements or purging voter rolls. Both Parties have also used tactics, such as setting strict voter ID requirements or purging voter rolls, which make it more difficult for certain groups to vote and gain any advantage in elections.

For example, the Republican Party has often supported strict voter ID laws, which require voters to present particular types of identification to vote. Voting rights advocates have criticized these laws for disproportionately affecting marginalized citizens such as minorities, low-income individuals, and older adults. They argue requiring voter IDs could make it more difficult for these groups to vote.

Accusers have claimed that the Democratic Party also engages in voter suppression tactics. For example, it has been claimed the Democratic Party has used absentee ballots to suppress voter turnout among certain groups of voters.

Voting rights advocates criticize voter suppression practices, arguing that they undermine the integrity of the electoral process. They also argue these tactics make it more difficult for certain groups of people to vote.

Increasing concern over the impact of partisanship on the American political system has led to efforts to promote bipartisanship and political cooperation. However, both Parties have often engaged in practices that sought to gain an advantage in elections by undermining the voting rights of certain groups. These practices have significantly contributed to the polarization and gridlock prevalent in American politics.

Voter identification laws and purges of voter rolls are controversial in the U.S., but none more so than the requirement for a physical ID. States design laws and regulations to ensure an election's integrity by verifying voter identities and maintaining accurate voter registration lists, which help prevent fraud and maintain the fairness of the electoral process. However, these measures can also disproportionately impact specific groups of voters, including minority communities and low-income individuals. Many criticize them as attempts to suppress the vote and undermine the democratic process.

The central argument for voter identification laws is that they help to prevent fraud by requiring voters to present a government-issued identification before casting a ballot. However, critics argue minority communities and low-income individuals are less likely to have personal identification.

For example, minority communities may be more likely to live in areas with inadequate access to driver's license offices or have difficulty obtaining the necessary documentation for government-issued identification. As a result, these laws can effectively disenfranchise voters and make it harder for them to participate in elections.

Purges of voter rolls, which involve removing the names of inactive or ineligible voters from voter registration lists, can also disproportionately impact specific groups of voters. States carry out voter purges to maintain the accuracy and integrity of voter registration lists. Still, they can also lead to eligible voters being removed from the rolls, particularly if they don't know there's a requirement to re-register or don't receive adequate notice. Purges can disproportionately impact minority communities and low-income individuals, who may be more likely to move frequently or have less access to information about the voter registration process.

Partisanship also plays a prominent role in the debate over voter identification laws and purges of voter rolls. Republican and Democrat lawmakers both support and oppose these measures in many cases, with each side often accusing the other of trying to manipulate the outcome of elections. This partisan division has contributed to a deeply divided and polarized political environment, with each side often viewing the other as trying to undermine the democratic process.

As mentioned, voter ID laws and purges of voter rolls can potentially impact the voting rights of specific Americans, particularly minority communities and low-income individuals. While some may intend these measures to ensure the integrity of elections, they can also have the unintended consequence of disenfranchising certain groups of voters and undermining the process. It's important for lawmakers to carefully consider these measures' potential impacts and ensure that all Americans have an equal opportunity to participate in elections to have their voices heard.

Gerrymandering, or manipulating the boundaries of electoral districts to give one political Party an advantage, was named after Elbridge Gerry, a prominent political figure in the early 19th century. Gerry served as a delegate to the Continental Congress and later as Governor of Massachusetts. He's perhaps best known for his role in gerrymandering, a tactic he used as a politician to manipulate the boundaries of electoral districts to benefit his political Party.

Gerry was born in Marblehead, Massachusetts, in 1744 and became involved in politics at an early age. He served in several important roles throughout his career, including as a Continental Congress member and Vice President under James Madison. As Governor of Massachusetts, Gerry was instrumental in implementing several reforms, including establishing a state board of education and creating a system of incorporating towns.

Gerry's often credited with inventing gerrymandering. Individuals or organizations typically achieve gerrymandering by drawing the boundaries of a district in such a way that it includes a disproportionate number of voters from one Party while excluding voters from the opposing Party.

In 1812, while serving as Governor of Massachusetts, Gerry signed a bill that redrew the State's electoral districts in a way that greatly benefited his Party. His redistricting plan was so blatant in its favoritism that it became known as the "Gerry-mander," and the practice of redistricting with bias became known as "gerrymandering" ever since.

While both political Parties have used gerrymandering throughout history, many consider it a corrupt and undemocratic tactic. Critics argue it undermines the integrity of the electoral process and allows politicians to choose their voters rather than the other way around. Despite these criticisms, gerrymandering remains a common practice in American politics and continues to be a source of controversy and debate.

The Party in power most often uses attempts at gerrymandering to maintain or increase its political dominance. Parties seek to create districts heavily skewed toward one Party or divide areas with many supporters of the opposing Party into multiple sections to dilute their voting power.

Parties can practice gerrymandering in several ways, including "packing," which involves concentrating the supporters of a particular Party into a few districts to minimize the number of communities they can win. Another way is "cracking," which divides the supporters of a specific Party into multiple sections to dilute their voting power.

In recent years, there's been increased attention and efforts to address the issue of gerrymandering in the U.S. Several States have implemented measures to reform the redistricting process to make it fairer and more democratic. Many people consider it a longstanding problem in American politics and criticize it for undermining the fairness and democracy of elections.

Several states have implemented measures to reform the redistricting process in response to these concerns. One example is California, which established an independent redistricting commission in 2010 to draw the State's electoral districts. The commission comprises five Democrats, five Republicans, and four independents and is responsible for drawing district lines that are neutral and fair.

Another example is Colorado, which adopted a ballot measure in 2018 that established a redistricting commission of four Democrats, four Republicans, and four independents. The Colorado commission draws the State's congressional and legislative districts fairly neutrally.

Other states implementing measures to reform redistricting include Arizona, Michigan, Missouri, and Utah. These States have adopted various approaches, including independent commissions, establishing redistricting standards and guidelines, and creating advisory committees to assist in redistricting. There continues to be increased attention and efforts to address the issue of gerrymandering. States continue to implement measures to reform the redistricting process and make it fairer and more democratic.

Party Organization

The two main political parties, Republican and Democrat, are organized at the national, state, and local levels and play a central role in the U.S. political system. They provide a means for individuals with shared political beliefs to come together and work toward common goals, such as influencing public policy and electing candidates to public office.

The primary purpose of the two major political Parties is to advocate for their respective political agendas and to promote the election of candidates who support those agendas. Democrats generally support progressive policies, including social justice, environmental protection, and access to healthcare, while Republicans support typically conservative policies, including lower taxes, less regulation, and smaller government.

Political parties are financed through individual donations, corporate contributions, and fundraising events. In the United States, there are limits on how much money individuals or organizations can contribute to political parties or candidates. The Federal Election Commission (FEC) sets these limits, which are subject to change over time. However, there also are disclosure requirements to ensure transparency. Disclosure has led critics to claim that wealthy donors and special interests influence the political system.

Political Parties also play a central role in selecting national political candidates in the United States. At the national level, Parties hold conventions every four years to choose their presidential nominees.

There are several other political parties in the United States besides the Democrats and Republicans. The Libertarian Party, for example, advocates for individual liberty, free markets, and non-interventionism. A left-wing party focusing on environmentalism, social justice, and nonviolence is the Green Party. The Constitution Party is a right-wing party that advocates for strict adherence to the Constitution and limited government. The Reform Party is a centrist party that aims to reduce the influence of special interests in politics and promote a more transparent and responsive government. These are just a few examples of the diverse range of political parties in the U.S.

Conventions, Primaries, and Caucuses

National political Party conventions are significant events that occur every four years in the U.S. to nominate a presidential candidate for the upcoming election. These conventions are open to all members of the Party and are an essential part of the democratic process.

Delegates to national conventions are chosen by various methods, depending on the rules of the Party and State where the representative resides. In some States, political parties or organizations choose delegates through a primary election or caucus, while the Party determines delegates in others.

Political parties or organizations typically choose convention delegates to represent the views and interests of the Party's members in their State or territory, regardless of the selection method. Once selected, delegates are responsible for casting votes at the convention to determine the Party's nominee for the presidential election. This process can be pretty complex, involving a series of polls and negotiations between different factions within the Party.

The first step in the nominating process is the roll call vote, in which each State's delegation announces the votes they're casting for each candidate. The convention typically bases these votes on the results of primary elections or caucuses held in the State. After the roll call vote, the convention naturally moves on to a series of ballots in which delegates vote for their preferred candidate.

The nomination is not necessarily determined on the first ballot, as it's common for no candidate to receive the required majority of votes. In this case, the convention may proceed to other polls, with delegates negotiating and making deals with one another to secure the necessary number of votes. This process can be intense and involves much behind-the-scenes maneuvering and horse trading.

Once a candidate has received the required number of votes, they're declared the nominee of the Party and will go on to represent their Party in the general election. The convention then concludes with a series of speeches. The nominee outlines their vision and plans for the future in an acceptance speech.

State and local Parties hold primary elections or caucuses to select candidates for various offices, such as senator, governor, and representative. These primaries are open to registered members of the Party and involve a series of votes to determine the Party's nominee.

Party members hold primary elections and caucuses to give them a say in who will represent their Party in the general election. These events allow voters to express their preferences and help narrow the field of candidates down to a single nominee. This caucus decision is critical when multiple candidates compete for the same office.

Primary elections and caucuses are typically open to registered members of the Party. This rule ensures that only Party members have a say in selecting the Party's nominee by only allowing individuals registered with the Party to participate in the voting process.

The primary election or caucus process involves a series of votes determining the Party's nominee. In a primary election, voters cast their ballots for their preferred candidate, and the candidate with the most votes is declared the nominee. In a caucus, voters gather in their local communities to discuss and debate the candidates before casting their votes.

Both primary elections and caucuses are an essential part of the democratic process, as they allow Party members to have a say in who will represent their Party in the general election. They allow voters to express their preferences and help ensure that the Party's nominee reflects the views and values of the Party's members.

Generally, State and local Parties hold primary elections or caucuses to select candidates for various offices, such as senator, governor, and representative. These primaries are open to registered members of the Party and involve a series of votes to determine the Party's nominee. Individuals organize the State and local Parties to advocate for their respective political agendas and promote the election of candidates who support them. They're financed through various sources and play a central role in selecting national political candidates through conventions and primary elections.

The political Party system in the United States has shaped the country's political landscape for over two centuries. However, the influence of wealthy donors and special interests has long been a source of controversy and criticism within the U.S. political system.

Critics of the Party system argue that it is heavily influenced by wealthy donors and special interests rather than focusing on the needs and concerns of ordinary citizens. Political Parties rely on financial contributions to fund their operations, often from wealthy individuals, corporations, and other special interest groups. Some argue that political Parties prioritize the interests of these wealthy donors and special interest groups over those of ordinary citizens and that these groups have disproportionate influence over the policies and positions of political Parties.

We can observe the influence of wealthy donors and special interest groups in how political Parties formulate their agendas and select their candidates. Since political Parties often rely on the support of big donors and special lobbies to fund their campaigns, candidates more supportive of these interests may be more likely to receive financial aid and ultimately be nominated. This influence can create a situation in which wealthy donors and special interest groups are more likely to fund candidates who align with their interests than candidates who represent ordinary citizens' needs and concerns.

Critics argue that wealthy donors and special interests significantly influence the U.S. political Party system by misusing campaign finance laws. They claim that these laws give the rich more control over the political process and that this influence undermines the democratic process.

In the United States, there are arbitrary limits on how much money individuals or organizations can contribute to political parties or candidates. However, there are also disclosure requirements to ensure transparency. Critics argue that wealthy donors disproportionately influence the political system by funding the campaigns of their preferred candidates. This inconsistency has led to criticism of the entire political. At the same time, critics argue the process often leaves out ordinary citizens.

The influence of wealthy donors and interest groups has resulted in a system that doesn't always prioritize the needs and concerns of the general public. Since the will of ordinary citizens is a vital part of the democratic process, addressing this issue is essential. Lawmakers and citizens need to consider ways to ensure that the political system is more representative of the needs and concerns of all Americans.

Lawmaker responsibility means eliminating barriers that prevent marginalized communities from participating in the political process and creating policies that address the citizenry's specific needs. Lawmakers can also ensure representation and responsiveness to more diverse needs by removing barriers and developing guidelines for marginalized communities' political participation.

For citizens, it's crucial to actively engage in the political process and hold elected officials accountable for their actions. This engagement includes participating in elections, attending town hall meetings, and making their voices heard through advocacy and grassroots organizing.

By being informed and active, citizens can help ensure that their representatives are responsive to their needs and concerns. They can also push for reforms that increase representation, such as redistricting reform and automatic voter registration. By working together, lawmakers and citizens can create a more representative political system that better serves all Americans.

Chapter 4

Citizenship, Rights, and Fights

There is often confusion and much discussion about what is and is not a Constitutional right. The U.S. Constitution defines four distinct types of rights. These are human (or natural), civic, civil, and political rights.

Human rights, or natural rights, are inherent to all human beings and aren't dependent on any particular society or government. Human rights include the right to life, liberty, and security of a person and the right to freedom of expression, religion, and association. Human rights are protected by international law and recognized as fundamental to the dignity and worth of every individual.

Many U.S. citizens misunderstand human rights for various reasons. Human rights are complex and multifaceted, encompassing many issues and values, such as the right to life, liberty, security, education, work, health care, freedom of expression, and religion. This complexity can make it difficult for people to understand the scope and significance of human rights entirely.

Another reason for the misunderstanding is the lack of education about human rights in the U.S. educational system. Some schools teach the basics of human rights but often overlook the depth and nuances in favor of other subjects. This insufficiency can lead to a limited understanding of the importance of human rights and the ongoing struggle to protect and defend them.

Contributing to misunderstandings about human rights is the perpetuation of myths and misinformation about the nature and purpose of these rights. For example, some people may believe that human rights are only relevant to particular groups or individuals or are only equally as crucial as nationalist interests, such as national security or economic development. These misperceptions represent a narrow and incomplete understanding of human rights as essential to the dignity and well-being of all individuals. All nations, states, and governments should respect and protect human rights globally.

One example in the U.S. is the controversy surrounding the misunderstanding of the rights of refugees and asylum seekers. Some people have criticized efforts to protect these individuals' rights, such as providing humanitarian assistance or resettling refugees within the United States, as unfair or dangerous to our security. Misinformation fuels the misunderstanding about the rights of refugees. Many people often overlook the importance of upholding our international obligations to protect human rights, instead adopting a position of nationalism.

The complexity of the topic, lack of education, and perpetuation of myths and misinformation often lead to a general misunderstanding of human rights. Individuals must educate themselves and support efforts to protect and defend these rights for all individuals, regardless of nationality.

Civic rights relate to the responsibilities and duties of citizens within a society. These rights include the right to participate in the political process, the right to hold public office, and the right to serve on a jury. Civic rights are essential to the functioning of a democratic society, as they allow citizens to actively engage in the decision-making processes that shape their communities and countries.

The term civic relates to the privileges and responsibilities of a community or country member. Civic rights often involve the right to participate in the political process and to engage in activities that contribute to the common good. Examples of civic rights also include the right to vote, the right to hold public office, and the right to serve on a jury.

On the other hand, civil rights are guaranteed to all individuals by law and protect individuals from discrimination based on specific characteristics, such as race, ethnicity, gender, and religion. Civil rights ensure that all individuals are treated equally and have the opportunity to participate fully in society. U.S. civil rights include equal protection under the law, freedom of speech, and a right to a fair and impartial trial.

The laws of a particular society or government protect civil rights. Civil rights may also include equal treatment under the law, the right to vote, and freedom from discrimination based on race, gender, and religion. U.S. national and State constitutions protect the Civil rights of the nation's citizens. This protection is essential for ensuring fair and equal treatment of all individuals. For example, one could argue that since U.S. citizen children under 18 don't have the franchise right to vote, they don't have all the same civil rights afforded to adult U.S. citizens. The franchise to vote is among the most important privileges extended to our nation's citizenry by our government. Voting in the United States is not a "right" of citizenship according to the word's definition because voting is conditioned upon an individual's circumstances and qualifications, other than one's citizenship. Citizenship is but one qualification that's needed to be extended the privilege to vote by the U.S. government.

U.S. citizens often misunderstand their civil rights for various reasons, including widespread misinformation. Another reason is that the history of civil rights in the U.S. is complex, with multiple movements and legislation addressing discrimination and inequality based on race, gender, religion, and other factors. This complexity has made it difficult for people to understand the scope and significance of their civil rights fully.

Another reason for the misunderstanding is a lack of education about civil rights in the U.S. educational system. History classes often teach the civil rights movement, but they often overlook the depth and nuance of the topic in favor of other subjects. This deficit can lead to a limited understanding of the struggles and triumphs of civil rights activists and the ongoing fight for equality.

Also contributing to misunderstandings about civil rights is the perpetuation of myths and misinformation about the nature and purpose of civil rights. For example, some people may believe that civil rights are only relevant to the past and that discrimination is no longer a significant issue in the United States. This belief is invalid, as discrimination and inequality remain substantial problems in American society. Civil rights are just as necessary today as they were in the past.

There are also misunderstandings about how civil rights apply to different groups. Some people may believe that civil rights are only relevant to certain marginalized groups, such as people of color or LGBTQ+ individuals. They may believe these rights don't apply to other groups. This belief constitutes a narrow and incomplete understanding of civil rights.

Another specific example of misunderstandings about civil rights is controversy surrounding advocacy groups such as the "Black Lives Matter" movement. Some have criticized the BLM movement as divisive or even racist, even though it's a grassroots effort to address the systemic racism and police violence African-American people face in the United States. Misformation and a lack of understanding about the history and purpose of the BLM movement fuel this misunderstanding.

U.S. citizens often misunderstand civil rights due to the complexity of the topic, a lack of education about civil rights, and the perpetuation of myths and misinformation. These misunderstandings are why it's essential for individuals to educate themselves about civil rights and to support efforts to promote equality and justice for all.

Finally, political rights relate to individuals' ability to participate in the political process and have a say in the decisions that affect their lives. Political rights include the right to vote, the right to run for public office, and the right to freely express and advocate for one's political beliefs. Political rights are critical to the functioning of a democratic society, as they allow individuals to have a voice in the decisions that shape their communities and countries. Many believe by denying millions of U.S. citizen children under age 18 the franchise right to vote, our nation's children don't have full political rights as are afforded to adult U.S. citizens. There's a shared belief regarding the millions of U.S. citizens living in the insular territories being denied voting representation in Congress. So, the quest for universal suffrage in the United States continues.

U.S. citizens often misunderstand their political rights for various reasons, including complexity. A big part is that the concept of political rights encompasses multiple issues and values. Values include freedom of expression, the right to vote, and the separation of powers. This complexity can make it difficult for people to fully understand the scope and significance of political rights.

Another reason for the misunderstanding is the lack of education about political rights in the U.S. educational system. Schools typically teach the basics, such as the structure of government and the role of the Constitution, but often overlook the nuances and complexities of political rights in favor of other subjects. This oversight can lead to a limited understanding of the importance of political rights and the ongoing struggle to protect and defend them.

Further contributing to this is the perpetuation of myths and misinformation about the nature and purpose of these rights. For instance, some may believe political rights are only relevant to particular groups or individuals. This lack of clarity represents a narrow and incomplete understanding of political rights essential to the functioning of a democratic society and the protection of individual freedoms.

Probably the most contentious example of misunderstandings about political rights is the controversy surrounding citizens' right to vote and how citizens exercise that right. Some people have criticized efforts to expand voting rights, like making voting more accessible through mail-in ballots or early voting, as unfair or undemocratic. People misunderstand the importance of providing equal opportunities for all citizens to participate in the political process. The spread of false information and a lack of knowledge on the topic are significant reasons for this misunderstanding.

In a democratic society, human, civil, civic, and political rights are essential to ensuring that all individuals are treated fairly and equally and can fully participate in their communities and country's political and social lives. The protection and promotion of these rights are essential to the functioning of a healthy and thriving democracy, and it's the responsibility of governments, citizens, and civil society organizations to work toward ensuring that all individuals have access to them.

Citizenship and Immigration

There are three main categories of citizenship status in the United States: immigrants, birthright citizens, and naturalized citizens. Each group has different rights and privileges regarding their civic, civil, and political rights.

Immigrants are defined as individuals who are living in the United States but who aren't U.S. citizens. They may be legally or illegally in the country with a visa or other permit. Immigrants generally have the same civil rights as U.S. citizens, protecting them against discrimination based on race, religion, and national origin. However, immigrants don't have the same political rights as U.S. citizens. Most notably, only qualified U.S. citizens have the right to vote in federal elections. Some U.S. States and local jurisdictions allow non-citizens to vote in certain local elections, but this is not the case in all parts of the country.

Birthright citizens are individuals who are U.S. citizens by being born in the United States or certain U.S. territories. Birthright citizens have all the rights and privileges of U.S. citizenship, including voting in federal elections. The Bill of Rights and other amendments to the U.S. Constitution also guarantee certain individual liberties, such as freedom of speech, religion, and the press for birthright citizens.

The laws of the United States govern the citizenship status of children born on foreign soil when at least one parent is a U.S. citizen. These laws, which have evolved, provide for the acquisition of U.S. citizenship by children born abroad in certain circumstances.

Under current U.S. law, a child born abroad to a U.S. citizen parent or parents may acquire U.S. citizenship at birth, generally under one of two conditions. One is if one parent is a U.S. citizen and that parent has lived in the United States for at least five years, at least two of which were after the age of 14. The other is that both parents are U.S. citizens, and at least one parent has lived in the United States for some time. Additional requirements apply in some cases, such as the need for the U.S. citizen parent to be physically present in the United States before the child's birth. Or the U.S. citizen parent needs a certain amount of financial support for the child.

It's important to note that the rules for foreign-born children acquiring citizenship at birth can be complex, and the specific circumstances of each case can affect the outcome. For example, the laws at the time of the child's birth may differ from those in effect today, which can affect the child's citizenship status. Additionally, the child's actions, such as obtaining a foreign passport or naturalizing as a citizen of another country, can impact their citizenship status.

In general, however, children born abroad to at least one U.S. citizen parent have a solid claim to U.S. citizenship. An immigration lawyer or a qualified expert can answer any questions about the citizenship status of a child born abroad to a U.S. citizen parent. Albeit mostly exceptional, there are other detailed conditions affecting the citizenship status of children born to U. S. citizens abroad.

Individuals can also become citizens through naturalization. They are known as naturalized citizens if they were not born in the United States. Naturalized citizens have the same rights and privileges as birthright citizens, including the right to vote in federal elections and the protection of the Bill of Rights and other amendments to the U.S. Constitution. However, there are a few exceptions.

For example, naturalized citizens who aren't yet 18 years old may not be eligible to vote, even if they meet all other requirements.

State laws also determine if naturalized citizens convicted of certain crimes lose their right to vote.

The United States also has several territories subject to its jurisdiction but aren't fully integrated into the Union. These territories, which include Puerto Rico, the U.S. Virgin Islands, Guam, and American Samoa, are home to millions of U.S. citizens by birth. However, the citizenship status of these individuals is not the same as individuals born or naturalized in one of the 50 states.

U.S. citizens who reside in territories are not considered citizens of the United States in the same manner as those born or naturalized in one of the 50 states. This determination means they don't have the same civil and political rights as citizens of the states. For example, residents of U.S. territories don't have the right to voting representation in federal elections and aren't represented in the U.S. Congress by voting members.

Despite their differences in citizenship status, Federal laws offer many of the same protections to residents of U.S. territories as it does to citizens of the states. For instance, the U.S. Constitution and federal civil rights laws protect them, and they can access many federal benefits and programs.

If a citizen of a territory moves to reside in one of the 50 states, their citizenship status doesn't change. However, they may gain additional civil and political rights due to their move. For example, if they become a resident of a state that allows them to vote in federal elections, they may be able to register to vote and participate in these elections. Additionally, they may be able to access certain benefits and programs only available to citizens of the states, such as specific financial aid programs or voting rights protections.

The citizenship status of individuals living in U.S. territories differs from those living in the 50 states. Although they may not have the same civil and political rights, they're still entitled to many protections under federal law. They can gain additional privileges if they relocate to one of the states.

Washington D.C., also known as the District of Columbia, is a unique jurisdiction in the United States. It's not a state, but it's not a territory, either. Instead, it's a federal district serving as the United States's capital.

As a federal district, the District of Columbia is not a part of any state and doesn't have the same citizenship status as the 50 states. However, like the territories, the District of Columbia is subject to the jurisdiction of the United States, and its residents are U.S. citizens.

Despite this, the District of Columbia has a unique civil and political rights status. For example, Federal laws offer most of the same protections to residents of the District of Columbia as to citizens of the states. Still, they do not have voting representation in national elections. They aren't represented in the U.S. Congress by voting members. This lack of voting representation has led to calls for the District of Columbia to become a state. As it has a population larger than some states, citizens are calling to give it voting representation in Congress.

In addition to its unique status, the District of Columbia has a special taxation status. As a federal district, the District of Columbia is not subject to federal taxes in the same way that the states are. Instead, it receives an annual payment from the federal government to cover the district's costs. The amount is the taxes the District of Columbia would have paid if it were a state. It is adjusted annually based on district population changes and other factors.

Since 2016, the District of Columbia has received an annual payment from the federal government equivalent to the taxes it would have paid if it were a state. In 2016, this payment was approximately $660 million. In 2017, it was roughly $675 million; in 2018, it was about $690 million. These amounts have helped to cover the costs of running the district and providing services to its residents.

Federal taxation of the citizens of the District of Columbia, also known as Washington D.C., has been a controversial issue for many years. As a federal district that's not a part of any state, the District of Columbia's unique taxation status has led to the argument that citizens of D.C. refer to as "taxation without representation." This viewpoint is that people shouldn't be required to pay taxes unless they have a say in using those taxes. This concept has a long history, dating back to the early days of the American colonies.

One of the most famous examples of taxation without representation occurred in the British colonies in America in the 1760s and 1770s, before U.S. independence. At that time, the British government imposed several taxes on the colonies, including the Stamp Act of 1765 and the Townshend Acts of 1767. These taxes presumably were to help maintain the colonies and protect them from foreign threats. Still, the colonists argued that they shouldn't have to pay these taxes because they had no representation in the British Parliament.

The slogan "no taxation without representation" became a rallying cry for the colonists, who used it to protest the taxes and demand more rights and freedoms. The slogan played a significant role in the lead-up to the American Revolution, and it's still remembered today as a fundamental principle of U.S. democracy.

Since the District of Columbia is not a state, its residents don't have the right to be represented in the U.S. Congress, but they're still subject to federal taxes. Many supporters of D.C. argue that this situation is unfair, advocating the district's residents should have the same rights as citizens of the 50 states. They point out that not only is the district home to a population larger than some states, but its residents also pay taxes just like citizens of the states do. They argue the district's residents should therefore have the right to vote in federal elections and to have their representatives in Congress. A compromise of sorts has recently been reached regarding three electors awarded to D.C. in the electoral college, exclusively for D.C.'s participation in selecting the president and vice-president, just as any other state. However, D.C. still has no voting representation in Congress.

Numerous efforts have been made over the years to address this issue by proposing to make the District of Columbia a state or give it voting representation. However, these efforts have faced significant opposition and have not succeeded. The district's unique taxation status and lack of representation in Congress have persisted.

In summary, the citizens' citizenship status in the District of Columbia is unique regarding their civil and political rights. They're U.S. citizens, but they don't have the same rights as citizens of the states. Additionally, the District of Columbia has a unique taxation status based on the annual payment it receives from the federal government to cover its costs.

Voting Rights Accorded by Status

Significant differences exist in the rights and privileges of immigrants, birthright citizens, and naturalized citizens in the United States. While the same civil rights laws protect all groups, there are essential differences in their political rights, particularly the right to vote in federal elections.

Immigrants in the United States generally have the same civil rights as citizens and protections against discrimination based on race, religion, and national origin. The Bill of Rights and other amendments to the U.S. Constitution guarantee certain individual liberties, such as freedom of speech, religion, and the press for immigrants.

There are some differences between immigrants and citizens regarding their political rights, including the right to vote. Only qualified U.S. citizens can vote in federal elections, although some states allow non-citizens to vote in certain local elections. These states and jurisdictions have chosen to extend voting rights to non-citizens to increase participation in local democratic processes and to recognize the contributions of non-citizens to their communities.

One state that allows non-citizens to vote in certain local elections is the State of Maryland. The laws of Maryland allow non-citizens who are legal permanent residents (also known as "green card" holders) to vote in local elections. In Maryland, the State grants non-citizens who have the right to live and work in the United States the right to vote in local elections.

Another jurisdiction that allows non-citizens to vote in local elections is the city of San Francisco, California. In San Francisco, non-citizens who are at least 18 years old, aren't in jail or on parole for a felony conviction, and have been a resident of San Francisco for at least 30 days are allowed to vote in local school board elections. This policy, in place since 2018, increases voter turnout and recognizes non-citizens' contributions to the community.

Chicago, Illinois, is another jurisdiction that allows non-citizens to vote in local elections. In Chicago, non-citizens at least 16 years old and city residents can vote for the city's community school boards in local elections. The policy, implemented in 2018, aims to engage more community members in the democratic process.

In Vermont, some towns and cities allow non-citizens to vote in local elections. Vermont law allows towns and cities to decide whether or not to allow non-citizens to vote in local elections. Several towns and cities in Vermont, including Montpelier, have allowed non-citizens to vote in local elections.

While the United States doesn't allow non-citizens to vote in federal elections, a few states and local jurisdictions have chosen to extend voting rights to non-citizens in certain local elections. These policies aim to increase participation in the democratic process and recognize non-citizens' contributions to their communities. Immigrants may also not be eligible to hold certain public offices or to serve on a jury.

Immigrants to the U.S. have many of the same rights as citizens, but there are some essential differences regarding their political rights and privileges. It's important to note that immigrants' rights can vary depending on their immigration status and the state's laws in which they reside. Some immigrants may be eligible for certain rights and protections that aren't available to others, while some may face additional restrictions or challenges.

The path to citizenship through naturalization is not always straightforward and involves some eligibility requirements. Some of the main requirements for naturalization include: Being at least 18 years old, being a permanent resident of the United States for at least five years (or three years if you're married to a U.S. citizen), being a person of good moral character, having a basic understanding of the English language, having a basic knowledge of U.S. history and government, and being willing to swear an oath of allegiance to the United States

In addition to these requirements, certain exceptions can disqualify an individual from becoming a naturalized citizen. For example, individuals convicted of certain crimes, such as murder or terrorism, are not eligible for naturalization. Additionally, we disqualify individuals from naturalization if they threaten national security or public safety. In the U.S., there's a distinction between regular immigrants and immigrants seeking asylum. Ordinary immigrants come to the United States for various reasons, such as working, studying, or being with family members. They may enter the United States with a visa or be eligible to apply for a visa once they're in the country.

On the other hand, immigrants seeking asylum are individuals fleeing persecution, violence, or other threats to their safety in their home countries. They may be eligible to apply for asylum in the United States if they show a well-founded fear of persecution based on race, religion, nationality, political opinion, or membership in a particular social group.

U.S. law grants certain protections regarding civil rights to regular immigrants and immigrants seeking asylum. For example, the U.S. Constitution and federal civil rights laws protect both groups, and both groups are entitled to due process of law and equal protection under the law.

There are differences in the rights and protections available to regular immigrants and immigrants seeking asylum. The United States may deport ordinary immigrants for violating their visa terms or being convicted of certain crimes. On the other hand, the government cannot deport asylum seekers with a well-founded fear of persecution in their home countries. Additionally, regular immigrants may not be eligible for certain benefits and protections available to asylum seekers, such as applying for work authorization or using certain forms of relief from deportation.

It's important to note that the naturalization process can be complex and may involve many other requirements and exceptions not listed here. Those interested in becoming a naturalized citizen should consult an immigration lawyer or a qualified expert for more information about the specific requirements that apply to their situation.

In contrast to the naturalization process, The United States automatically grants birthright citizenship to specific individuals born in the United States or citizens born abroad to U.S. citizen parents. This rule means that if you're born in the United States or if you meet specific other requirements, you may be able to become a U.S. citizen without going through the process of naturalization.

Immigration and Paths to Citizenship

There are only two main paths to citizenship in the United States: birthright citizenship and naturalization. Birthright citizenship is automatically granted to specific individuals, while naturalization is the process by which an individual who is not a U.S. citizen can become a citizen. Many requirements and exceptions apply to both of these paths, and it's essential to understand them to determine which approach is correct.

Both naturalized citizens and birthright citizens have the same civil rights, which are protections against discrimination based on race, religion, and national origin. The Bill of Rights and other amendments to the U.S. Constitution guarantee both groups certain individual liberties, such as freedom of speech, religion, and the press.

There are critical differences between naturalized citizens and birthright citizens regarding their political rights, including the right to vote. Most naturalized citizens have the same right to vote as birthright citizens, but a few exceptions exist. For example, naturalized citizens who aren't yet 18 years old may not be eligible to vote, even if they meet all other requirements. Depending on state laws, the government can revoke the right to vote for naturalized citizens convicted of certain crimes. There are some differences between naturalized citizens and birthright citizens regarding their rights. Both groups are generally entitled to the same legal protections and privileges.

Interestingly, there are a few non-traditional ways that an individual can become a citizen of the United States. One such method is through a process called "derivative citizenship." A person becomes a citizen through a parent's naturalization or acquisition of citizenship. In contrast, the person is still a minor.

Another nuanced way is through the "acquisition of citizenship at birth." This option occurs when a person is born outside the United States to a U.S. citizen parent or parents and acquires citizenship at birth. This circumstance can happen if the parent or parents meet specific physical presence requirements in the U.S. before the child's birth.

An individual can also become a citizen through the "resumption of citizenship." This circumstance occurs when a person was previously a U.S. citizen but lost citizenship due to renouncing citizenship or serving in a foreign country's armed forces and reacquiring citizenship.

Birthright or naturalization are the most common ways to become a citizen. Derivative citizenship, acquisition of citizenship, or the resumption of citizenship are non-traditional and less common ways to become a citizen. It's important to note that these non-traditional ways of becoming a citizen exist.

On the other hand, there are also several ways a U.S. citizen can lose their citizenship. One way is through renunciation, in which a person voluntarily and intentionally gives up their U.S. citizenship. To renounce citizenship, an individual must appear before a U.S. consular or diplomatic officer and formally renounce citizenship.

Another way to lose citizenship is through expatriation. This situation occurs when the U.S. government terminates citizenship. An individual can renounce their allegiance to the United States by performing actions such as serving in a foreign country's armed forces, voting in a foreign election, or seeking and obtaining foreign naturalization.

It's worth noting that, for expatriation to be effective, the individual must intend to give up their U.S. citizenship. This qualification means that an individual who performs one of the above actions without an intention to renounce their U.S. citizenship will not lose their citizenship.

One example of a person who lost their citizenship through renunciation is John Walker Lindh, an American who was captured during the war in Afghanistan and subsequently renounced his U.S. citizenship. Another example of citizenship lost through expatriation is Edward Snowden, the former National Security Agency contractor who leaked classified information and sought asylum in Russia.

Laws and practices that disproportionately affected minority groups, including naturalized citizens, have been used throughout history in the United States to suppress the right to vote. These discriminatory practices violate the principles of justice and equality in our democratic society.

One example of a practice disproportionately affecting minorities was the English literacy requirement, stating that an individual had to be able to read and write in English to vote. This requirement disproportionately affected many naturalized citizens, represented by immigrants from countries where English wasn't the primary language. Local and State governments often used this requirement to suppress the vote of naturalized citizens and other minority groups. The practice was finally eliminated through the Voting Rights Act of 1965.

Other voter suppression tactics include purging voter rolls, implementing strict voter identification laws, and closing polling places in predominantly minority neighborhoods. These tactics have been shown to affect minority groups, including naturalized citizens, disproportionately and can make it more difficult for them to exercise their right to vote.

Declaring Independence

The rights of citizens of the U.S. have long been a contentious issue between the citizens and their government. For instance, the rights to "life, liberty, and the pursuit of happiness" are commonly considered rights guaranteed in the original U.S. Constitution. However, the right to "life, liberty and the pursuit of happiness" was originally written by Thomas Jefferson in June 1776 and is found in the "Declaration of Independence," not the original U.S. Constitution.

The "Declaration of Independence" document that the Continental Congress adopted on July 4, 1776, declared the 13 colonies in North America to be independent of the British Empire. The Declaration of Independence justifies the colonies' decision to break away from Britain as a statement of principles rather than a legally binding document. One of the fundamental principles outlined in the Declaration is the idea that all people are entitled to certain unalienable rights, including "life, liberty, and the pursuit of happiness."

Enlightenment philosophy influenced the belief that inherent rights were rights no government or authority could take away. The Declaration asserts that these rights are given to all people by their "Creator," and governments exist to protect them. The philosophy of "Enlightenment" was an intellectual movement during the late 1700s, emphasizing reason, individualism, and liberty. This philosophy significantly influenced those who drafted the U.S. Constitution, and many ideas can be traced back to Enlightenment thinkers.

A key idea from the Enlightenment that influenced the content of the U. S. Constitution was the concept of natural rights, which are rights believed to be inherent to all individuals, regardless of the laws or customs of a particular society. The Enlightenment philosophers thought these natural rights, such as the right to life, liberty, and the pursuit of happiness, were fundamental and couldn't be taken away by the state.

The Enlightenment also emphasized the importance of limited government and the separation of powers. The U.S. Constitution reflects this idea by dividing the federal government into three branches (legislative, executive, and judicial) and establishing a system of checks and balances to prevent any branch from gaining too much power.

Lastly, the Enlightenment stressed the importance of individual liberty and protecting the rights of the minority from the majority's tyranny. The Constitution reflects this idea through the Bill of Rights, which lists rights protected from government infringement, such as freedom of speech, religion, and the press. Enlightenment philosophy continues to influence the way the United States governs today.

While the Declaration of Independence recognizes the unalienable rights of "life, liberty, and the pursuit of happiness," the Constitution of the United States, the highest law of the land, doesn't explicitly mention happiness. Instead, the U.S. Constitution focuses on protecting the rights of life and liberty. It sets forth a system of government and establishes certain rights and protections for the citizens of the United States. It also lays out the powers and responsibilities of the three branches of government and sets forth the procedures for amending the document.

The framers of the Constitution omitted the mention of the pursuit of happiness because they did not intend it to be a comprehensive Statement of all of Americans' rights and freedoms. Instead, it creates a framework for the government to protect certain fundamental rights. The founders of the United States believed that the pursuit of happiness was a natural right, a human right, not a civil right, so it didn't need to be specifically enumerated in the Constitution.

In addition, the Declaration of Independence has no standing in the legal system. It's not legally binding and doesn't have the force of law. Instead, it serves as a Statement of principles, a historical document that reflects the ideals and values of the founders of the United States.

After the Civil War, Congress adopted several measures to protect individual rights from interference by the States. One of the most important measures was the 14th Amendment, adopted in 1868.

The 14th Amendment prohibits the States from depriving "any person of life, liberty, or property, without due process of law." This prohibition means that the States aren't allowed to take away an individual's life, liberty, or property without following the legal procedures established by law.

Widespread civil rights abuse during the Civil War and Reconstruction periods prompted the adoption of the 14th Amendment. During this time, many States passed laws that restricted the rights of African-Americans and other minority groups, including laws that denied them the right to vote, hold public office, and own property. The 14th Amendment provides a constitutional safeguard against these abuses by requiring the States to respect the fundamental rights of all individuals.

The 14th Amendment has also significantly impacted the protection of individual rights in the United States. The courts have used the 14th amendment to strike down State laws that violate an individual's rights and to extend federal protections to the States. For example, the Supreme Court has used the 14th Amendment to invalidate State laws that discriminate based on race, gender, and other forms of discrimination.

The 14th Amendment is an integral part of the Constitution. It prohibits the States from depriving "any person of life, liberty, or property, without due process of law." It was adopted to protect the rights of individuals from interference by the States and has played a crucial role in protecting individual rights in the United States.

Age Discrimination and Children's Rights

The 26th Amendment to the U.S. Constitution, adopted in 1971, lowered the minimum voting age in the U.S. from 21 to 18. This amendment was a significant milestone in the history of the United

States' voting rights, as it granted young people the right to vote on an equal basis with adults.

Young people below age 21 were denied because many believed they weren't mature enough or responsible enough to make informed decisions about political issues. However, this view was widely challenged during the 1960s, as young people became more politically active and demanded the right to vote. The Vietnam War was also an important motivator.

The movement to lower the voting age argued it was unfair to deny people the right to vote simply because of their age. They pointed out that young people under 21 were considered mature enough to be drafted into military service, pay taxes, and be tried as adults before U.S. courts; therefore, they should be allowed to vote.

Despite resistance from some quarters, the movement for a lower voting age eventually convinced Congress to adopt the 26th Amendment. The States ratified this amendment in 1971, granting young people between the ages of 18 and 21 the right to vote on an equal basis with adults.

The 26th Amendment significantly impacted the political landscape of the U.S. It allowed young people to participate in the democratic process and have a voice in the decisions that affect their lives. It's also helped to ensure that at least some of the nation's young people are treated equally under the law, and it's paved the way for further progress in the fight for civil rights and equality, most especially voting rights for the nation's children.

The 26th Amendment was an important milestone regarding "age-defined" rights. Unfortunately, age-based discrimination still affects many, especially the nation's youngest citizens.

U.S. law defines children as "fully formed human beings under 18." It grants them the same fundamental constitutional rights as adults. Unfortunately, the law hasn't always been applied consistently. The legal definition of children's rights includes the right to freedom of speech, freedom of religion, and the right to due process under the law. However, the law recognizes that many children are not physically and emotionally mature enough to handle the responsibilities that come with other legally recognized activities of citizenship. So, U.S. law has developed several mechanisms to reconcile this recognition with the need to protect children and ensure they aren't taken advantage of or exploited. Still, it doesn't treat them equally to other adult citizens. Historically, U.S. laws have denied children the franchise privilege of suffrage, or as it's more commonly known today, the "right to vote."

U.S. law addresses this "citizen age" issue through what is defined to be the citizen's "age of majority." The age of majority is a legal term initially reserved to States' rights, and that refers to the age at which a person is legally capable of making decisions and exercising their rights. In most States, the age of the majority is 18. States consider a person an adult at this age, and they can enter into contracts, vote, and make other legal decisions.

State law determines the age of the majority in the United States, which is considered a "state's right." This consideration means that each state can set its age of majority individually and may establish different ages for different rights and responsibilities.

For example, in some states, the age of majority for entering into contracts is 18, while in others, it's 21. This rule means that in states where the age of majority for contracts is 18, an individual who is 18 or older is legally able to enter into a contract, while in states where the age of majority is 21, an individual must be 21 or older to enter into a contract.

Other rights and responsibilities that may be affected by the age of majority include the ability to vote, serve on a jury, and join the military. In some states, the age of majority for these rights is 18, while in others, it's still 21.

In addition to the age of majority, other periods of legal majority apply to specific rights and responsibilities. For example, the legal drinking age in the United States is 21, which means that individuals must be 21 or older to purchase and consume products containing alcohol.

While the age of majority is 18 in most States, there are some exceptions to this rule. In some States, a person may be able to enter into certain types of contracts or make certain legal decisions at a younger age. Additionally, some States have established different ages of majority for various legal activities. For instance, a person may be able to vote at 18 but may not be able to purchase alcohol until the age of 21.

Similar to the ages of majority established by States' rights, the 14th and 26th Amendments define them too. These Amendments are often used to develop the concept of an "age of majority," recognizing a belief that children are not yet fully mature while affording them mostly the same fundamental constitutional rights as adults. In principle, this acknowledges that children should gradually gain more responsibility and independence as they grow and develop while protecting them from exploitation and abuse. Unfortunately, this creates an ambiguity in U.S. law that has often been inconsistently and arbitrarily applied to the nation's children.

The 26th Amendment to the U.S. Constitution responded to the political and social climate of the late 1960s. As young people increasingly participated in civil rights, and anti-war movements and demanded the right to vote, it became increasingly necessary to address this issue.

The 26th Amendment argues for eliminating age discrimination in the United States. By granting 18-year-olds the right to vote, the amendment recognized the age young people are capable of making informed decisions and participating in the democratic process. An example of legal ambiguity is that this same logic can apply to the workplace, where age discrimination prevents individuals from fully contributing their skills and talents.

The minimum age for joining the U.S. military is 17 with parental consent or 18 without parental consent. This rule means that individuals who are at least 17 years old and have the permission of their parent or guardian can enlist in the military, while those who are 18 or older can join without the need for parental consent.

The minimum age to vote in the United States is 18. This voting rule means all individuals 18 or older can register to vote and participate in elections.

It's worth noting that the minimum age for joining the military is still lower than the minimum age for the right to vote. This fact exemplifies another ambiguity. It establishes that a young citizen might be mature enough to fight for or otherwise serve their country, perhaps even sacrifice their life for their country, without concomitantly having the right to participate in the nation's democratic process by voting.

Adult U.S. military and other service members can cast ballots to vote the same way as other U.S. citizens, with a few additional considerations. For instance, military and other service members stationed within the United States can register to vote and cast their ballots like other citizens, either in person at their polling place on Election Day or by absentee ballot if they cannot vote in person.

Military and service members serving in foreign countries have a few additional options for casting their ballots. One option is to use the Federal Voting Assistance Program (FVAP), a program administered by the Department of Defense that helps military and overseas citizens register to vote and request an absentee ballot.

Another option is to use the Overseas Vote Foundation (OVF), a non-profit organization that provides voting assistance to U.S. citizens living abroad. The OVF website includes information about registering to vote, requesting an absentee ballot, and casting a ballot from overseas.

Modern Discrimination and Inequality

Title VII of the Civil Rights Act of 1964 prohibits employment discrimination based on race, color, religion, sex, and national origin. While this act doesn't specifically mention age, the U.S. Equal Employment Opportunity Commission (EEOC) has interpreted it as prohibiting age discrimination against individuals who are 40 years or older.

The "Age Discrimination in Employment Act of 1967 (ADEA)" protects against age discrimination for individuals 40 or older. This act specifically prohibits employers from discriminating against employees based on age in hiring, promotion, pay, and other terms and conditions of employment.

Together, the 26th Amendment and these two acts provide solid legal protection against age discrimination in the U.S. By using these laws; individuals might argue that age discrimination is not only wrong but also illegal or in violation of their constitutional rights.

The 26th Amendment, Title VII of the Civil Rights Act of 1964, and the Age Discrimination in Employment Act of 1967 might someday be used to argue for the elimination of age discrimination in voting in the U.S. These laws ensure that individuals of all ages receive fair and respectful treatment both in the workplace and public spaces.

Discrimination and inequality remain significant problems in American society for many reasons. The legacy of systemic racism and segregation in the United States for much of its history is just one reason. The 13th Amendment formally abolished slavery in 1865, but discrimination against racial and ethnic minorities continues to impact U.S. society today.

Another reason is the ongoing existence of explicit and implicit biases in U.S. society, which can lead to discriminatory treatment of certain groups. While most forms of clear bias are recognizable, implicit biases are unconscious attitudes or stereotypes that can influence one's actions and decisions. Bias can be challenging to recognize or acknowledge by law. Yet, bias can manifest in our communities in various ways, such as through discriminatory hiring practices, unequal access to education and other resources, and discriminatory treatment by law enforcement.

Contemporary Fights for Rights

The passage of the Civil Rights Act of 1964 and the Voting Rights Act of 1965 were significant milestones in the fight for civil rights. Yet discrimination and inequality continue to be substantial problems in American society. Decades after laws were passed, people continued to fight for civil liberties granted by them. The "Black Lives Matter" movement was formed in 2013 and is an example of one such fight. The "BLM" movement was created in response to the shooting of Trayvon Martin and focuses on racial justice and police brutality.

Other examples of the continuing struggle for civil rights include the fight for LGBTQ+ rights, indigenous people's rights, and the rights of immigrants and refugees. These struggles highlight the ongoing need for efforts to address discrimination and inequality in American society.

The fight for LGBTQ+ rights is about ongoing efforts to ensure that lesbian, gay, bisexual, transgender, and queer individuals can enjoy the same rights and protections as other members of U.S. society. These rights include a right to marry, a right to employment and housing, and a right to protection from discrimination and violence.

One example of a fight for LGBTQ+ rights is marriage equality. Before the U.S. Supreme Court's decision in Obergefell v. Hodges in 2015, same-sex couples weren't allowed to marry in many states. This decision, which legalized same-sex marriage nationwide, was a significant milestone in the fight for LGBTQ+ rights.

Another example is the fight for employment and housing protections for LGBTQ+ individuals. While federal law prohibits discrimination based on sex, it doesn't explicitly protect against discrimination based on sexual orientation or gender identity. Many states still allow firing or denying housing to LGBTQ+ individuals based on their sexual orientation or gender identity. Efforts are ongoing to pass laws that protect LGBTQ+ individuals in these areas.

Finally, the fight for LGBTQ+ rights also includes efforts to address violence and discrimination against LGBTQ+ individuals. These efforts include attempts to pass hate crime laws that specifically protect against crimes motivated by bias against LGBTQ+ individuals, as well as efforts to address discrimination and violence against transgender individuals, particularly transgender women of color. The fight for LGBTQ+ rights is an ongoing effort to ensure that all individuals can enjoy the same rights and protections, regardless of their sexual orientation or gender identity.

Another civil rights fight being waged is for the nation's Indigenous people, as an ongoing effort to protect the rights, cultures, and ways of life of U.S. Indigenous peoples. Activists fight to recognize and protect Indigenous peoples' lands and to ensure their right to self-determination and treatment with respect and dignity.

An example of the fight for indigenous rights is the ongoing struggle to recognize and protect indigenous lands. In the U.S., indigenous peoples have historically been dispossessed of their ancestral lands through various means, including colonization, forced removal, and land-grabbing. Efforts are ongoing to secure the recognition and protection of indigenous lands, including establishing indigenous-controlled territories and negotiating new treaties and agreements with the U.S. government.

Another example is the fight for the right to self-determination, which includes the right of indigenous communities in the U.S. to determine their own political, economic, social, and cultural development. Self-determination consists of the right to govern themselves, the right to control their resources, and the right to preserve their cultures and traditions.

The fight for indigenous rights in the U.S. also includes efforts to address discrimination and violence against indigenous individuals and communities. These efforts include addressing issues such as police brutality, the overrepresentation of indigenous people in the criminal justice system, and the lack of access to education, healthcare, and other essential services.

Taken together, these fights for indigenous rights in the U.S. are an ongoing effort to ensure that indigenous peoples can enjoy the same rights and protections as other members of U.S. society while preserving and protecting their cultures, traditions, and ways of life.

The civil rights fight for the rights of immigrants and refugees in the U.S. is an ongoing effort to protect their rights and well-being.

This effort includes the fight for fair and humane immigration policies, the right to due process, and the right to respect and dignity.

One example of the fight for the rights of immigrants and refugees in the U.S. is for fair and humane immigration policies. These policies include efforts to reform the immigration system to provide a pathway to citizenship for immigrants living in the U.S. without documentation and to protect the rights of refugees and asylum seekers.

Another example is the fight for immigrants and refugees to have the right to due process, which includes a fair and impartial hearing before an immigration court. This fight is also about their right to legal representation, the right to present evidence, and the right to appeal a decision. Much controversy exists in the U.S. about recognizing certain civil rights for the nation's immigrants and refugees.

The fight for the rights of immigrants and refugees in the U.S. is an ongoing struggle that also includes efforts to address discrimination and mistreatment of immigrants and refugees. This effort includes eliminating discrimination in the workplace, in housing, and by law enforcement. Recognition of immigrant and refugee rights in the US aims to ensure these groups have the same rights and protections as others in U.S. society and promote a more fair and just society.

Equal Protection

The Equal Protection Clause is a fundamental part of the 14th Amendment to the U.S. Constitution. As previously mentioned, the 14th Amendment was adopted in the aftermath of the Civil War as part of the Reconstruction Amendments. The clause ensures equal treatment and non-discrimination by the government for all people within the United States.

The 14th Amendment's Equal Protection Clause states that "no state shall ... deny to any person within its jurisdiction the equal protection of the laws." This statement means the government must provide equal protection under the law to all individuals within its jurisdiction, regardless of race, ethnicity, national origin, religion, gender, sexual orientation, or disability. The clause prevents the government from enacting laws or policies that discriminate against certain groups of people or treat individuals differently based on these characteristics.

The United States has applied the Equal Protection Clause in significant cases throughout history. One of the most famous examples is the 1954 Supreme Court case, Brown v. Board of Education, which ruled that segregation in public schools violated the Clause and was therefore deemed unconstitutional. The Court held that segregation had a detrimental effect on African-American children and denied them equal educational opportunities. This decision was a significant victory for the U.S. civil rights movement. It helped pave the way for further racial equality in the nation, including, perhaps, the future voting rights of its children.

In recent years, the U.S. has applied the Equal Protection Clause in cases related to LGBTQ+ rights. In 2015, the Supreme Court ruled in Obergefell v. Hodges that the Clause required states to allow same-sex couples to marry and to recognize same-sex marriages performed in other states. This decision marked a significant step forward in the fight for LGBTQ+ equality and extended the rights and protections previously afforded only to opposite-sex couples to same-sex couples.

The 14th Amendment's Clause ensures that the nation's government treats all individuals within the jurisdiction of the United States equally and without discrimination. This clause is critical in protecting all individuals' rights and ensuring fairness and justice for all.

It's easy to take for granted that children in the U.S. are afforded the same legal protections as adults, but this isn't always the case. Historically, the U.S. has treated children as their parents' property and denied them the same legal rights as adults. The 14th Amendment and its Equal Protection Clause recognizes children as individuals deserving of rights and protections under the law. Still, as has often been the case in the U.S. regarding extending certain rights to marginalized groups, there is much work to be done in establishing enforcement of children's rights, with the most significant part of the difficulty firmly founded in issues of States' rights. As with other rights struggles in U.S. history, children's rights must be hard fought to win.

The Equal Protection Clause guarantees equal treatment and prohibits discrimination by the government against all individuals within the jurisdiction of the United States. While it's clear that this clause applies to adults, there has been much debate over whether it should also apply to the nation's children.

People have made several arguments for excluding children from consideration based on the Equal Protection Clause. Some argue the adult proxy is based on children's mental and emotional development as incomplete, so they cannot fully comprehend or exercise their rights. Some claim that children need their parents' or guardians' guidance and protection because they cannot make informed decisions.

Yet, the U.S. holds children to adult standards before the law. People commonly argue that children should not be held to the same legal standards as adults since they're not entirely responsible for their actions. Yet, children as young as nine have been tried as adults in U.S. courts. People often use this "maturity" argument to justify excluding children from the protection of the Equal Protection Clause, which prohibits states from denying any person "equal protection of the laws."

It's true that children are not fully developed mentally or emotionally and may not always fully understand the consequences of their actions. Nevertheless, U.S. courts and society hold them to adult standards before the law. This circumstance seemingly creates a double standard unfair to children and can have severe consequences for their future and the nation.

For example, case precedent establishes children as young as 13 have been tried as adults in certain criminal cases based on the state and the severity of their offense. The rulings subjected children charged with a crime to the same penalties as adults, including imprisonment. In some cases, trying children as adults can send them to adult prisons, putting them at risk of physical abuse and other dangers.

Another example of U.S. society holding children to adult standards is the sentencing of children to life in prison without parole. U.S. law sentences children convicted of certain crimes to spend the rest of their lives in jail, regardless of age or potential for rehabilitation. This application of U.S. law contradicts the "age of majority" standard applied elsewhere in our laws, the same standard afforded as a State's rights consideration. It's another ambiguous, inconsistent application of U.S. law that abridges certain U.S. citizens' civil liberties. This question of age discrimination in the civil rights of children establishes a need to clarify, perhaps Constitutionally define, the rights of the nation's children. Children don't enjoy the full civil rights and protections of citizenship as afforded to the population of U.S. adult citizens.

The arguments that children aren't fully accountable for their actions and shouldn't be held to the same standards as adults are problematic. While it's essential to recognize that children aren't fully developed and may not always fully understand the consequences of their actions, it's also vital to ensure that children are treated fairly and justly under the law. We create a double standard when excluding children from the protection of the Equal Protection Clause or applying the Clause arbitrarily or inconsistently by holding children to adult standards before the law. This wavering of inclusion and exclusion of the nation's civil rights protections of children, seemingly at the legal "whimsy" of our Courts, is unfair and ultimately counterproductive. It is also extraordinarily unjust.

Arguments about an "age of majority" and a child's mental fitness to participate in the democratic process may seem compelling, but ultimately, they're flawed. A "mental fitness" qualification standard for voting was once similarly applied to the nation's formerly enslaved people. Children are individuals with individual rights and needs. They shouldn't be allowed to treat children as the property of their parents or the property of the state. All individuals deserve dignity and respect. Arbitrarily excluding children from the Equal Protection Clause of the 14th Amendment is unjust and goes against the country's fundamental principles of fairness and equality.

Some citizens today advocate allowing children to participate in the democratic process without being held to the aforementioned "age of majority" or a mental fitness standard. One view is that children have the same fundamental constitutional rights as adults and, therefore, should have the right to vote. The 26th Amendment grants young people, recognized as fully-fledged citizens based on age, the right to vote. By lowering the voting age from 21 to 18, the U.S. allowed younger citizens to have a say in the direction of their country. Still, some feel it's time to reexamine the benchmark for recognizing an age of majority based upon the principles of an evolving and maturing society's culture.

It's important to remember that children are the country's future and are affected by the decisions made by adult citizens and the government. Denying them the right to participate in the democratic process is a disservice to them and the country's future. Furthermore, it's again important to note the U.S. currently holds children to adult standards before the law, that children today work and pay taxes just like adults, and that arbitrarily excluding them from the protection of the 14th Amendment's Equal Protection Clause is unjust. It goes against the country's fundamental principles of fairness and equality. All individuals, including children, deserve dignity and respect, and the Equal Protection Clause is an important reason the 14th Amendment was drafted and ratified. It protects these rights for all U.S. citizens, regardless of their age.

Chapter 5

We Need Money

Money plays a critical role in the success of a political party's or candidate's election campaign. Without sufficient funds, it's difficult for parties and candidates to effectively get their message out to the public and compete with their opponents. There are many different areas in which money is essential in political campaigns, and understanding these can help better understand money's role in the electoral process.

One of the most obvious ways money is essential in political campaigns is through advertising. Parties and candidates must get their message out to persuade voters to support them. This need often requires paying for advertising space in various media outlets, such as television, radio, newspapers, online platforms, and billboards. The more money a party or candidate has, the more advertising they can afford, and the more effective they'll be in getting their message out to the public. Adequate financial resources can give them a significant advantage over their opponents, particularly if they have fewer financial resources.

Another way money is essential to political campaigns is by hiring a candidate's campaign staff. Parties and candidates often need to hire professionals to manage their campaigns, such as fundraisers, strategists, and field organizers. By paying staff members for their time and expertise, parties or candidates can run their campaigns more effectively and with more staff members. Money also enables hiring more or better qualified and experienced personnel. For example, a party or candidate with more campaign staff may be able to reach out to more voters, coordinate more campaign events, and develop more sophisticated campaign strategies.

Money is also crucial in covering travel costs for candidates and campaign staff. Candidates and their staff often must travel to different parts of the country to attend campaign events and meet with voters. Money is needed to cover the costs of transportation and accommodation. The more money a party or candidate has, the more resources they'll have for travel and the more places they'll be able to visit. This ability can be crucial in large, geographically diverse countries like the U.S., where it may be necessary to travel long distances to reach potential voters.

In addition to the more obvious ways money is essential, there are many other areas where it can make a difference in a political campaign. For example, parties and candidates may need to pay to produce campaign materials, such as flyers, brochures, and yard signs. These materials are essential for getting a candidate's or campaign's message out to the public. These materials can be costly to produce in large quantities.

Parties and candidates may also need to conduct polls to gauge public opinion and inform their campaign strategies or use data analytics to target their messages to specific voter groups. Many campaigns now use social media to reach voters, and this often involves paying for targeted advertising. Finally, parties and candidates may hold fundraising events to collect money for their campaigns, which can be expensive to organize and may also require the rental of venues, catering, and other expenses.

Money plays a critical role in the success of a political party's or candidate's election campaign. While money's not the only factor determining an election's outcome, it's crucial. Parties and candidates with more financial resources can often run more effective campaigns and reach more voters, giving them a significant advantage over their opponents. At the same time, it's essential to recognize that there are limits to money's role in politics. Other factors, such as the quality of a party's or candidate's platform and the strength of their organization, can also be important in determining the outcome of an election.

Platforms and Campaigns

A political platform is a set of positions or principles a political party advocates for an individual candidate. Platforms guide the policies and actions the party or candidate will take if elected. These platforms can cover various issues, including economic policy, healthcare, education, foreign policy, criminal justice, and social issues.

The party or candidate's core values and beliefs are central to most political platforms. These fundamental principles guide their actions and decisions, including positions on individual freedom and liberty, social justice and equality, or limited government intervention in people's lives. These principles help shape the party or candidate's policy positions and governance style.

Policy positions are vital elements of political platforms. Positions are specific proposals for how the party or candidate addresses particular issues, such as healthcare, education, or the economy. Policy positions range from broad, sweeping reforms to more targeted, specific proposals. They often reflect the party or candidate's core values and beliefs and can be a critical factor in attracting voter support.

In addition to policy positions, political platforms may outline the party or candidate's vision for governance and leadership. Their platform can include how they make decisions, communicate and collaborate, and their views on government and the private sector's role. Voters perceive a party or candidate's governance style, which can significantly impact their level of support.

Budget and spending priorities are other vital elements of political platforms. Parties and candidates often outline how they plan to allocate resources, including which areas they plan to invest in and which they plan to cut. Planning can be a critical factor in attracting voter support, as it helps to give voters a sense of the party or candidate's priorities and values.

Political reform is another element included in political platforms. Parties and candidates may propose changes to the political system, such as campaign finance reform or modifications to the electoral process.

It's important to emphasize that political platforms are essential to any political campaign. They typically include core values and beliefs, policy positions, governance and leadership style, budget and spending priorities, and political reform. These elements help to give voters a sense of the party or candidate's priorities and values. Platforms can be a critical factor in attracting voter support.

How About Some Political Action

Political Action Committees, or PACs, raise and spend money to elect or defeat political candidates. The Federal Election Campaign Act of 1971 authorized PACs in the United States, setting limits on campaign contributions and creating the Federal Election Commission (FEC) to oversee the campaign finance process.

The Federal Election Campaign Act of 1971 (FECA) is a United States federal law regulating campaign finance, including raising and spending money in national elections. The Federal Election Campaign Act of 1971 also addresses concerns about money's influence on politics and lack of transparency in campaign finance.

The primary purpose of FECA is to increase transparency in campaign finance and limit the amount of money raised and spent in federal elections. It does this through several provisions, including limiting campaign contributions, establishing disclosure requirements, and prohibiting specific donations.

FECA is supposed to limit the amount of money individuals, political committees, and other organizations can contribute to candidates, parties, and political action committees (PACs). Presumedly, this helps to prevent wealthy donors from exerting undue influence on the political process. FECA requires candidates, political parties, and PACs to reveal their campaign funding sources and how they use funds. This information is made available to the public through the Federal Election Commission (FEC) when appropriately disclosed. Enforcement is problematic. Moreover, the wealthy and special interests have found loopholes in FECA that allow them to circumvent the law's intentions.

In addition to setting limits on contributions and establishing disclosure requirements, FECA also prohibits certain types of donations, such as those from foreign nationals or those made in another person's name. These requirements supposedly help ensure the campaign finance process is fair and transparent.

FECA also established the Federal Election Commission (FEC) as an independent government agency to oversee the campaign finance process. The FEC is responsible for enforcing FECA and regulating campaign finance, including enforcing contribution limits and disclosure requirements. It discloses campaign finance information to the public and guides candidates, parties, and PACs on campaign finance laws and regulations.

The Federal Election Campaign Act of 1971 (FECA) is a critical law aiming to increase transparency in U.S. campaign finance and limit money's influence in the nation's politics. It does this through contribution limits, disclosure requirements, and prohibiting specific contributions. The Federal Election Commission (FEC) plays a crucial role in enforcing FECA and regulating campaign finance.

The general purpose of PACs is to raise and spend money in support of, or opposition to, political candidates, parties, or issues. Political Action Committees (PACs) can affiliate with a specific political party, interest group, or cause. For example, some PACs support environmental causes, labor unions, and gun rights.

Corporations, associations, and other groups can also form PACs to promote or oppose specific issues or candidates.

Individuals, organizations, and corporations fund Political Action Committees (PACs) through contributions. Federal law limits how much PACs can contribute and requires them to disclose their funding sources. Some states also have laws regulating PACs and campaign finance.

Types of PACs include separate segregated funds (SSFs), affiliated with corporations or unions, and nonconnected committees (NCCs), not affiliated with any particular organization or corporation. SSFs must use the money they raise for specific purposes, such as to support candidates or issues, while nonconnected committees have more flexibility in how they can use their funds.

Strict rules and regulations, including disclosure requirements and limits on fundraising and spending, apply to Political Action Committees (PACs). These rules ensure transparency and prevent undue influence on the political process. Again, enforcement is problematic because it primarily relies on disclosures, which may or may not be forthcoming, timely, or truthful.

Disclosure requirements and limits on fundraising and spending are some critical rules and regulations that apply to Political Action Committees (PACs). One of the most important rules is about disclosing their funding sources.

Federal law also requires PACs to disclose the names of individuals, organizations, and corporations that contribute more than $200 annually. The Federal Election Commission (FEC) makes this information public. Disclosure requirements help ensure transparency in the campaign finance process and prevent secret or hidden funding sources from influencing elections.

In addition to disclosure requirements, PACs are also subject to limits on how much money they can raise and spend. Federal law limits the amount of money contributed to PACs and the amount PACs can spend on elections. These limits help to prevent wealthy donors or special interest groups from exerting undue influence on the political process.

In addition to the rules and regulations that apply to PACs, some restrictions apply to other political committees, such as candidate and party committees. These committees are also subject to disclosure requirements and limits on how much money they can raise and spend.

Designers of rules and regulations for Political Action Committees (PACs) intend to ensure transparency and prevent undue influence in the political process. Disclosure requirements help ensure that sources of PAC funding are known. Requirements help limit the amount of money raised and spent and are supposed to help prevent wealthy donors or special interest groups from having too much influence. PAC rules are an essential part of the campaign finance system in the United States, which helps ensure that U.S. elections are fair and democratic. Unfortunately, the rules don't always work to that end.

In addition to raising and spending money to support or oppose candidates and issues, PACs can also engage in other political activities, such as voter education and registration efforts or research and policy analysis. They can also engage in grassroots lobbying, influencing legislation through direct contact with policymakers and the public. This practice is highly controversial.

PAC organizations collect and distribute campaign contributions to candidates for political office, regulated by the Federal Election Commission (FEC). According to the FEC, PACs can only contribute a limited amount of money to candidates for federal office.

During the 2020 election cycle, PACs could contribute up to $5,000 to a candidate per election (primary and general elections count as separate elections). In addition, PACs are not allowed to contribute directly to presidential campaigns. Still, they can contribute to other committees that support presidential candidates, such as the Democratic National Committee or Republican National Committee (FEC, 2020).

Another important rule for PACs is that they can only make independent expenditures to support or oppose candidates. The Federal Election Commission (FEC, 2020) states that independent expenditures are communications that advocate for or against a candidate not coordinated with the candidate's campaign. This rule means that PACs cannot coordinate directly with a candidate's campaign on ads or other forms of communication that support or oppose the candidate.

The Federal Election Commission (FEC) requires PACs to disclose their contributions and expenditures in addition to other rules. Disclosures include information on the amount of money they have received and spent, the recipients of their expenses, and the purposes of their expenditures (FEC, 2020). This transparency is essential to ensure the public understands how PACs spend their money and who they support or oppose.

There are also rules governing the types of contributions that PACs can accept. For example, PACs cannot accept contributions from foreign nationals or federal government contractors (FEC, 2020). They also cannot accept donations in cash or checks over $100 (FEC, 2020). These rules are in place to prevent foreign influence and corruption in the political process.

Generally, PACs are subject to many other rules governing how they can spend their money and ensure transparency and fairness in the U.S. political process. These rules include limits on contributions to candidates, further restrictions on independent expenditures, and requirements for disclosure of contributions and expenses.

By following the rules, PACs can play a valuable role in financing political campaigns while also upholding the integrity of the electoral process. Unfortunately, PAC participation hasn't always met that lofty goal or FECA's intent. The primary purpose of FECA is to increase transparency in campaign finance and limit the amount of money raised and spent in federal elections, but it often falls short.

Look, We're On TV

Television advertising has played a significant role in political campaigns in the United States since the 1950s. With the widespread adoption of television as a primary source of entertainment and information, political campaigns quickly recognized the potential of television advertising to reach a large and diverse audience. Over the years, television advertising has evolved in content, production values, and targeting, but it remains an essential tool for political candidates seeking to get their message out to voters.

One of the earliest examples of television advertising in a political campaign was Dwight D. Eisenhower's "I Like Ike" ad in 1952. This ad featured a simple slogan and catchy jingle that helped to build support for Eisenhower's campaign.

In 1964, the campaign of Lyndon B. Johnson effectively used television advertising by airing the "Daisy" ad. This ad featured a young girl picking petals off a daisy, followed by a countdown and an image of a nuclear explosion. This ad implied that Johnson's opponent, Barry Goldwater, was reckless and would lead the country into a nuclear war.

Over the years, political campaigns have continued to use television advertising to reach voters. Some of the most effective ads have been memorable and captured the audience's attention. For instance, the re-election campaign of Ronald Reagan in 1984 effectively used the "Morning in America" ad. It featured images of everyday Americans going about their lives, set to a positive and uplifting musical soundtrack. By featuring photos of the lives of ordinary Americans, the re-election campaign effectively used the ad to create a sense of optimism and hope.

On the other hand, there have been many examples of television ads that were ineffective or even counterproductive for political campaigns. During George H.W. Bush's 1988 campaign, they featured the "Willie Horton" ad, highlighting a convicted murderer released on a weekend furlough program in Massachusetts.

The campaign of George H.W. Bush intended to attack his opponent, Michael Dukakis, for being soft on crime by featuring the "Willie Horton" ad. Many criticized it as racist and fear-mongering despite the campaign's intention of attacking the opponent, Michael Dukakis, for being soft on crime. A group supporting the campaign of George W. Bush in 2004 ran "Swift Boat" ads that attacked the military service of the opponent, John Kerry, and many criticized the ads as misleading and dishonest.

As previously stated, television advertising has played a significant role in political campaigns in the United States since the early 1950s. While some ads have effectively communicated a campaign's message and built support for a candidate, others have been ineffective or counterproductive. As political campaigns continue to use television advertising to reach voters, it will be necessary for candidates to carefully consider the content and messaging of their ads to communicate with the public effectively.

Radio advertising is another media format that's played a significant role in political campaigns in the United States. Radio has been used since the 1920s when it emerged as a mass medium. With its ability to reach a large and diverse audience, radio advertising quickly became an essential tool for political candidates seeking to get their message out to voters. Over the years, radio advertising has evolved in terms of its content, production value, and targeting, but it remains an essential tool for political campaigns.

The campaign of Al Smith in 1928 used one of the earliest examples of radio ads in political campaigning through the use of what's known as the "Radio Priest" ad. This ad featured Father Charles Coughlin, a popular radio personality, who supported Smith's campaign. The campaign of Franklin D. Roosevelt in 1944 effectively used radio advertising by airing the "Fala" ad. The campaign aimed to humanize Roosevelt and appeal to voters emotionally by featuring his dog, Fala, in the ad. Children and pets have been a recurring theme within political campaign advertising in the U.S.

Over the years, U.S. political campaigns have continued to use radio advertising to reach voters, but with the advent of the Internet, radio has fallen somewhat out of favor. Some of the most influential radio ads have been well-written, memorable, and captured the audience's attention. For instance, the campaign of Richard Nixon in 1952 effectively used a radio address as an example of political advertising, in which Nixon defended himself against allegations of financial impropriety by using what's remembered as the "Checkers" ad. Many people credit the "Checkers" ad for helping Nixon win the election. This Nixon ad is still recognized as one of history's most influential.

On the other hand, there have been many examples of radio ads that were ineffective or counterproductive. A group supporting the campaign of George W. Bush in 2004 ran a series of radio and television ads, known as the "Swift Boat" ads, which attacked the military service of the opponent, John Kerry. Many criticized these ads as misleading and dishonest.

Radio advertising has played a significant role in political campaigns in the United States since the 1920s, and it continues to do so today. While some ads have effectively communicated a campaign's message and built support for the candidate, others have been ineffective. Political campaigns must carefully consider the content and messaging of their ads to communicate effectively.

Another campaign ad resource is print media advertising, including newspaper and magazine advertising. These forms of advertising have played significant roles in political campaigns in the U.S. since the Republic's early days. Today, political campaigns use print media as an essential tool to reach specific audiences and deliver targeted messages. But television and digital advertising have primarily overshadowed the print media in recent years.

One of the earliest examples of print media advertising in a political campaign was the "Join or Die" cartoon, which appeared in the Pennsylvania Gazette in 1754. This cartoon, which depicted a snake divided into segments representing the colonies, was used to rally support for forming a unified colonial government. Another early example of print media advertising was the "Handbill" campaign of John Adams in 1800, in which Adams and his supporters distributed pamphlets attacking the character and policies of his opponent, Thomas Jefferson.

Today, digital media advertising, including the internet, social media, and mobile devices, plays an important role in political campaign advertising. Digital media has been around in the United States since the late 1990s. With the rapid growth of the internet and the proliferation of digital devices, political campaigns have increasingly turned to digital advertising as a way to reach voters. Digital advertising through social media also offers several advantages for political campaigns, including targeting specific demographics, tracking ad effectiveness, and delivering real-time messages.

The campaign of Al Gore in 2000 used one of the earliest examples of digital media advertising in a political campaign through the "I Approved This Message" ad. Al Gore's campaign aimed to appeal to voters personally by featuring Gore speaking directly to the camera in the "I Approved This Message" ad. Another early example of effective digital media advertising was the "Hope" ad campaign of Barack Obama in 2008. This ad featured images of Obama set to an uplifting soundtrack and was widely credited with helping Obama win the election. The "Hope" ad became one of U.S. history's most iconic political ads.

Over the years, political campaigns have continued using digital media advertising to reach voters. Some of the most effective ads have been well-produced, visually appealing, and captured the audience's attention. The campaign of Hillary Clinton in 2016 effectively used the "Stronger Together" ad, an example of political advertising which featured a montage set to a positive and inspiring soundtrack. Hillary Clinton's 2016 ad helped to create a sense of unity and hope by featuring a montage of everyday Americans set to a positive and inspiring soundtrack using the slogan "Stronger Together." Many credited this ad for Clinton's win in the popular vote.

Digital media advertising has played a significant role in political campaigns since the 1990s. While some ads have effectively communicated a campaign's message and built support, others have been counterproductive. As political campaigns continue to use digital media to reach voters, candidates will increasingly need to consider the content and message of their ads.

Generally speaking, many forms of advertising have played significant roles in the political campaign since the Republic's early days. From print ads in newspapers and magazines to radio and television ads to digital advertising on the internet and social media, candidates have used various forms of advertising to communicate their messages and build support. Again, some of the most effective ads have been well-written, memorable, and captured the audience's attention. This goal is the adopted model for political advertising. Ineffective, counterproductive ads still exist due to misleading or dishonest content or failure to communicate effectively with the public. The effectiveness of advertising in political campaigns has varied over time. Many factors affect an ad's effectiveness, including content, the medium used, and the cultural context presented.

Campaign to the Stars

Celebrities and iconic figures have played a significant role in United States political campaigns since the Republic's early days. Campaigns have often sought the endorsement of celebrities and other iconic figures to build their support and credibility. These endorsements can take various forms, like television ads, social media posts, and public appearances.

One of the earliest examples of advertising endorsements in a political campaign was the "Lincoln-Douglas Debates" in 1858, in which Abraham Lincoln and Stephen Douglas, the two candidates for the U.S. Senate in Illinois, engaged in a series of public debates. While these debates were not technically "advertising," they were widely covered by the media and helped elevate both candidates' profiles.

In 1932, Franklin D. Roosevelt's campaign ran the "Celebrity Cavalcade" ad, an early example of celebrity endorsements. This ad featured a series of approvals from prominent figures, including actors, athletes, and business leaders, who spoke in support of Roosevelt's campaign. It was highly effective in getting Roosevelt elected.

Over the years, political campaigns have continued to use celebrity endorsements as a way to reach voters. The most effective endorsements are those genuine, sincere, and aligned with the candidate's values and priorities. It doesn't hurt to get the endorsement of an influential celebrity, either. For example, Oprah Winfrey's endorsement of Barack Obama in 2008 widely helped him win the election. The "Oprah endorsement" validated Obama's message of hope and change.

On the other hand, there are many examples of celebrity endorsements that were ineffective. For instance, the endorsement of Charlie Sheen for Donald Trump in 2016 was widely criticized as inappropriate and lacking in credibility. Similarly, the endorsement of Kid Rock for Donald Trump in 2020 was widely criticized as divisive and out of touch.

As political campaigns continue to seek the endorsement of celebrities and other iconic figures, it will be necessary for candidates to carefully consider the impact and alignment of these endorsements with their campaigns. With the advent of digital social media, campaigns are being introduced to a new era of advertising opportunities.

It's All in the Cards

Signage, handbills, bumper stickers, pins, and other similar items have also played a role in U.S. political campaigns. These materials usually promote a candidate or party and sometimes carry slogans to persuade potential voters to support a campaign.

One of the earliest forms of political signage was handbills, also known as flyers. The early practice was distributing them publicly, but mailing them to potential voters later was common. Handbills and flyers could present information about a candidate or party's platform or attack an opponent. Early campaigners used handbills to reach a broad audience. For a long time, most people didn't have access to television or other forms of mass media, as are common these days.

Bumper stickers emerged as a popular political advertising tool in the 20th century. Stickers could be easily attached to the bumper of a car and were a visible way to show support for a particular candidate or party. Like other forms of political advertising, bumper stickers effectively convey a message by promoting a candidate's name or campaign slogan.

Another popular form of political advertising has been using hats and caps, t-shirts, pins, and buttons. These items have been used in campaigns for many years and are often given out at rallies or events to show support for a particular candidate or party. These items can effectively convey a message as they're usually worn and seen in public spaces.

There have been many examples of effective and ineffective political signage, handbills, bumper stickers, pins, and other similar items throughout the history of political campaigns in the United States. Some examples of effective signage-type ads have included the "I Like Ike" bumper stickers used in Dwight Eisenhower's 1952 presidential campaign and the "Hope" posters featuring Barack Obama during his 2008 presidential campaign. Both of these items effectively promoted the candidate and captured the attention of potential voters.

It's Mostly a Rally

Political rallies have long been a staple of political campaigns in the United States. Rallies serve various purposes, including providing a platform for candidates to speak to large groups of people, energizing supporters, and attracting media attention.

The first political rallies in the U.S. were held in the early 19th century and were often used to mobilize support for a particular candidate or party. These early rallies were usually held in public squares or on the steps of government buildings and attended by large crowds.

Over time, political rallies have evolved to include various elements, such as speeches by candidates, music, and other forms of entertainment. Political campaigns often hold rallies in large venues like arenas or stadiums, frequently televising or broadcasting them on the radio. They're often used for fundraising and typically offer various indirect benefits to participants in exchange for their campaign donations. The object is to influence the electorate's vote.

There have been many examples of effective and ineffective political rallies throughout the history of political campaigns in the United States. Some examples of effective rallies include the "Change We Can Believe In" rally held by Barack Obama during his 2008 presidential campaign and the "Morning in America" rally held by Ronald Reagan during his 1984 presidential campaign. These rallies effectively mobilized support for the candidate and energized their supporters.

On the other hand, there have also been examples of ineffective political rallies. Violence and disruptions marred Donald Trump's "Make America Great Again" rally during his 2016 presidential campaign, making it useless in persuading voters. Critics criticized Mitt Romney's "Restore Our Future" rally during his 2012 presidential campaign for its lack of enthusiasm and energy.

Political rallies have played a role in political campaigns in the United States. Poor planning or execution of rallies can make them ineffective. However, if done well, rallies can mobilize support and energize supporters.

Rallies have grown in importance in recent years, becoming an effective way for candidates to mobilize support and energize their supporters. The modern era of technology allows rallies to be broadcasted to an even larger audience through live streaming and social media coverage, making it easier for candidates to reach a wider audience. Additionally, in recent years, rallies have become more frequent and expansive in scale, with more candidates using them to kick off their campaigns and rally supporters just before an election. The increased number of rallies demonstrates their importance as a tool for political campaigns.

A Web of Dos, Don'ts, and Maybes

The Internet has played a significant role in political campaigns in the United States since it became widely available in the late 20th century. It has provided a new platform for candidates to reach potential voters and revolutionize campaigns.

Bill Clinton's 1996 presidential campaign was the first to use the Internet. During this campaign, the Clinton campaign used email to communicate with supporters and to raise funds. Since then, the Internet has become an increasingly important tool for political campaigns, with candidates and parties using it for various purposes.

Political campaigns use the Internet for various purposes, including fundraising, voter outreach, and campaigning. Candidates and parties often use social media platforms such as Twitter™ and Facebook™ to communicate with potential voters and to promote their campaigns. They also use websites and email to communicate with supporters and to fundraise.

There have been many examples of effective and ineffective uses of the Internet in political campaigns in the United States. One example of effective use was Barack Obama's 2008 presidential campaign, which extensively used social media and emails to mobilize support and raise funds. Obama's campaign reached many potential voters using various media channels, which was a significant factor in his victory.

There have also been examples of ineffective uses of the internet in political campaigns. Critics argued that the 2016 Hillary Clinton presidential campaign's reliance on data analytics and targeted advertising didn't effectively reach or persuade voters. In the 2020 election, critics found the spreading of misinformation and conspiracy theories online by the presidential campaign of Donald Trump harmful to the democratic process.

The Internet has provided a new platform for candidates to reach potential voters and revolutionize campaigns. However, it has also been criticized for its potential to spread misinformation and harm the democratic process.

Another tool, called data analytics, has played a significant role in forming political platforms in recent years. Political parties and candidates use data analytics to gather and analyze information about potential voters to better understand their preferences and concerns. Campaigns use this information to inform the development of their platforms and messaging.

An example of the successful use of data analytics in forming a political platform was the 2008 presidential campaign of Barack Obama. The Obama campaign extensively used data analytics to gather information about potential voters and target their messaging and outreach. Obama used data to identify potential supporters, tailor campaign messaging to specific groups, and target fundraising efforts. The Obama campaign's use of data analytics was a significant factor in its success.

There have also been examples of unsuccessful uses of data analytics in the formation of political platforms. Critics criticized the 2016 presidential campaign of Hillary Clinton for relying too much on data analytics and targeted advertising. Some argued the Clinton campaign's use of data analytics didn't effectively reach or persuade voters and may have contributed to her defeat.

While data analytics can be an effective tool for gathering information about potential voters and targeting outreach, it can also be misused or fail to reach or persuade voters effectively. Political parties and candidates must use data analytics responsibly and consider various factors when developing their campaign platforms using data analysis metrics.

Political platforms use many methods to model and analyze voter behaviors other than through data analytics. Political parties and candidates often use various techniques to gather information about potential voters and develop their campaign platforms.

Public opinion polls and focus groups are standard methods used in most political campaigns. These techniques involve surveying a population sample or gathering a group to discuss and provide feedback on specific issues or candidates. Political parties and candidates can better use the results of these polls and focus groups to understand potential voters' concerns and preferences and inform the development of their campaign platforms.

Another method used in the formation of political platforms is the use of policy experts and advisors. Political parties and candidates often seek the input of experts in specific policy areas to develop informed and well-crafted policy positions. This can include consulting with academics, think tanks, and other organizations specializing in particular policy issues.

There have been many successful and unsuccessful uses of these methods by political platforms. One example of the successful use of public opinion polls and focus groups was the 1992 presidential campaign of Bill Clinton. Clinton's campaign used these techniques to understand voters' concerns better and craft a platform that resonated with the broadest cross-section of the population. Political analysts credited this technique as a significant factor in Clinton's victory.

Examples exist of unsuccessful uses of these methods too. For instance, the 2000 presidential campaign of George W. Bush faced criticism for relying too heavily on a small group of advisors and not seeking input from a broader range of policy experts. Their method contributed to a few unpopular policies and decisions made during the Bush administration.

As mentioned previously, many methods other than data analytics are used to form political platforms. These methods can effectively gather information about potential voters and develop informed policy positions. They can also be misused or fail to consider the concerns and preferences of voters effectively. It's proven important for political parties and candidates to use various methods in forming their platforms to ensure that they're well-informed and responsive to the needs of voters.

A politician's unique purpose is a specific goal or agenda that that politician seeks to achieve through their political career. This purpose can include various issues, such as advancing policies, promoting social justice, or advocating for specific groups or interests.

There have been many examples of people who were not U.S. politicians successfully achieving their particular political purpose in life. One example is Martin Luther King Jr., who used his ministerial career to advocate for civil rights and racial equality. King's efforts played a critical role in the civil rights movement and the eventual passage of the Civil Rights Act of 1964 and the Voting Rights Act of 1965.

Another successful non-politician with a particular political purpose was Susan B. Anthony, who dedicated her career to advocating for women's rights and suffrage. Anthony's efforts played a significant role in the passage of the 19th Amendment, granting women the right to vote.

On the other hand, there have also been examples of non-politicians who were unsuccessful in achieving their unique political purpose. One example was the abolitionist John Brown, who led a failed raid on the federal armory at Harpers Ferry to end slavery. Brown's efforts were unsuccessful, and the conflict over slavery continued until the Civil War.

Chapter 6

Reform School

Have you ever felt like your opinions and views have little influence on the decisions made by the government? You could be right. A Princeton University study, "Public Opinion Has 'Near-Zero' Impact on U.S. Law," (Page, 2014) provides a comprehensive analysis of the role of public opinion in shaping U.S. law and policy. The study, by Professors Martin Gilens (Princeton University) and Benjamin I. Page (Northwestern University), analyzed data from more than 1,800 policy issues from 1981 to 2002. The study found that the views of ordinary Americans have almost no influence on the laws and policies the U.S. government enacts.

A key finding of the study is that the number of Americans for or against any particular idea has no impact on the likelihood that Congress will make it law. In other words, laws and policies are passed and implemented without considering the views of the majority of Americans. Instead, the study found the opinions of wealthy Americans and powerful interest groups are much more likely to shape the laws and policies of the U.S. government.

The Princeton study found that the wealthy and powerful's views tend to prevail over the general public's. This finding is factual even when the general public's views are firmly held and widely supported. The study also found that the general public's views are more likely to be represented in policy only when they align with those of the wealthy and powerful.

In addition to its findings on the limited impact of public opinion on U.S. law and policy, the Princeton study also highlights the role of media in shaping public opinion. It explores how the media can be influenced by the wealthy and powerful.

Over time, the media has played an enormously significant role in shaping public opinion and the decisions made by the nation's government and other institutions. Media outlets, such as news organizations and social media platforms, are many people's primary sources of information. They can influence how people think and feel about various issues.

A way in which the media can shape public opinion is through the selection and presentation of news stories. Media outlets can decide which stories to cover and how to cover them, and these choices can considerably impact how people view the world. For instance, if a media outlet consistently covers stories about crime in a particular neighborhood, it can create the impression that the area is dangerous, even if crime rates are low. Similarly, if a media outlet focuses on negative aspects of a particular issue or event, doing so can negatively shape public opinion.

In addition to selecting and presenting news stories, the media can shape public opinion through language and framing. How a story is written or presented can influence how people interpret and understand it. For example, if a media outlet consistently refers to a group of people as "illegal immigrants," it can create negative associations and shape public opinion.

The media can also be influenced by the wealthy and powerful. This influence can occur through the use of advertising and other forms of media manipulation. For example, suppose a wealthy individual or interest group wants to promote a particular policy or candidate. In that case, they may use advertising and other forms of media to shape public opinion. In some cases, influential individuals or interest groups directly own or control media outlets, which can further distort the information presented to the public. The Princeton study also found that media coverage of policy issues skews in favor of the views of the wealthy and powerful and that this bias can significantly impact the general public's opinions.

Princeton's study provides a sobering assessment of the role of public opinion in shaping U.S. law and policy. Its findings support the assertion that the views of ordinary Americans have little impact on the laws and policies enacted by the U.S. government and that the opinions of the wealthy and powerful are much more likely to shape the country's direction. These findings demonstrate the importance of democratic governance and reveal the need for reforms to include the general public's views in the policy-making process.

The Princeton and Northwestern professors analyzed more than two decades' worth of data to investigate whether or not the U.S. government represents the people. They were alarmed to discover that the concerns and issues of 90% of Americans virtually do not affect government actions and policies.

Political corruption uses political power for personal or financial gain and has become a significant problem in contemporary U.S. politics. Corruption can take many forms, including the abuse of power, the misuse of public funds, and the influence of special interests.

One form of political corruption is an abuse of political power. This abuse can include politicians using their positions to make decisions that benefit themselves or their friends and allies rather than influencing the public good. This circumstance can have serious consequences, such as misallocating public resources or eroding trust in the political system.

Another form of political corruption is the misuse of public funds. Corruption can include politicians using public funds for their benefit or funneling money to friends and allies through contracts or other means. This condition can lead to waste and inefficiency and undermine the political system's integrity.

The influence of special interests is another form of political corruption. Influence can include politicians swayed by campaign contributions or other support from powerful interest groups. This influence can result in decisions that benefit those special interests rather than the broader public.

Sadly, there have been many examples of political corruption in contemporary politics. One high-profile example is the Watergate scandal, involving power abuse by members of the Nixon administration. The Jack Abramoff lobbying scandal is an example of special interests influencing politics and resulted in several politicians' convictions for corruption.

Some might argue political corruption is a significant problem in U.S. politics today. It can take many forms and have serious consequences, including the abuse of power, the misuse of public funds, and influence by special interests. Politicians and the public need to be vigilant in combating political corruption. They should work together to ensure the political system is transparent and accountable.

Political reform movements are groups or organizations that advocate for changes to the political system to address perceived problems or injustices. These movements often promote transparency, accountability, and fairness in the political system and may suggest various reforms to achieve these goals.

Political reform movements have a long history in the United States. One example is the progressive movement of the late 19th and early 20th centuries, which sought to address corruption, economic inequality, and social justice. This movement led to some critical reforms, including establishing the direct primary system, the initiative and referendum process, and the passage of the 19th Amendment, which granted women the right to vote.

Another example of a political reform movement is the civil rights movement of the 1950s and 1960s, which sought to address racial segregation and discrimination issues. This movement led to many necessary reforms, including the Civil Rights Act of 1964 and the Voting Rights Act of 1965.

Political reform movements often suggest a variety of reforms as needed in the U.S. political system. These can include measures to promote transparency and accountability, such as campaign finance reform and stricter disclosure requirements for politicians and lobbyists. Other reforms may address representation and fairness issues, such as redistricting reform and measures to increase voter turnout.

In general, political reform movements are groups or organizations that advocate for changes to the political system to address perceived problems or injustices. These movements have led to many necessary reforms. Reform movements often suggest a variety of reforms as needed in the U.S. political system.

Citizens have also directly identified several critical areas of concern in the U.S. political system and have proposed reforms, such as extending voting rights to all regardless of age or geographic residential location. These reforms also address issues related to U.S. elected representation in Congress, campaign financing, and other common concerns about the political system in the United States.

Ranked Choice: Fixing Broken Elections

Ranked-choice voting is an electoral system in which voters can rank candidates in order of preference. This system ensures that the majority of voters' order of importance is in the winner of an election, not just the candidate with the most votes. In ranked-choice voting, voters can rank candidates in order of preference on their ballot. The candidate who receives the most votes is declared the winner unless there are not enough votes for them to be considered the majority. We eliminate the candidate with the fewest votes and reallocate their votes to the remaining candidates based on the voters' preferences. This process is ranking candidates by voter choice.

Ranked-choice voting originates from the late 19th century as a proposal to address "spoiler" election candidates. In a ranked-choice system, these candidates are less likely to split the vote and disrupt the election, as voters can rank them lower on their ballots.

The purpose of ranked-choice voting is to provide a more democratic and representative outcome in elections. It allows voters to express their preferences more fully and ensures that the winner of an election reflects the preferences of the majority.

There are some arguments both for and against ranked-choice voting. Proponents argue it's a more democratic and representative system, allowing voters to express their preferences. Ranked-choice voting reduces the need for negative campaigning by incentivizing candidates to appeal to a broader range of voters rather than just their base.

On the other hand, critics argue that ranked-choice voting can confuse voters and may result in lower turnout. Implementing it can also be more expensive, requiring more advanced voting equipment and software.

In summary, ranked-choice voting can be fairly described as an electoral system that allows voters to rank candidates in order of preference. Ranked choice provides a more democratic and representative outcome in elections, but it can also be confusing for voters and more expensive to implement. Whether it's better or worse than the present system depends on the specific context and the priorities of the voters and policymakers involved.

Transparency to End Gerrymandering

Gerrymandering is drawing electoral district boundaries in a way that unfairly benefits one political party or group. Creating districts with a heavily concentrated number of voters from one party or splitting up areas with many voters from the opposing party can achieve this.

Gerrymandering can have significant consequences for the fairness and integrity of the electoral process. It can lead to the dilution of the voting power of certain groups and the exaggeration of the influence of others, resulting in a distorted representation of the will of the voters.

There are several options for addressing gerrymandering and promoting more accurate representation for all voters. One option is the creation of independent, fully transparent redistricting commissions. We can use these tools to create more compact and contiguous districts that better reflect the demographic and political makeup of the region. Policies could include requirements to consider population size, geography, and community interests rather than just political considerations.

Another option is using algorithms or other objective tools to draw electoral district boundaries. States can use these tools to create districts that reflect the region's demographic and political makeup, making them more compact and contiguous. Overall, gerrymandering is a practice that can have significant consequences for the fairness and integrity of the electoral process. Measures can help ensure that the will of the voters is reflected in the political system by actively promoting accurate representation for all voters, regardless of the political party.

Inclusive Voting in Primaries

One potential reform for the electoral process is adopting a single, open primary controlled by voters, in which all candidates for the same political office compete. This system would allow voters to choose the candidates appearing on the ballot rather than having the political Party establishment select them through a closed primary or convention process.

There are some potential benefits to this approach. First, it gives voters more control over the electoral process. By allowing them to choose the candidates who will appear on the ballot directly, voters can have a more significant say in the nation's direction and the issues emphasized during the campaign.

Second, this system can provide more choices on the ballot. By allowing all candidates to compete in the same primary, voters can consider a broader range of candidates and may be more likely to find candidates who align with their views. This system can lead to more diverse and representative candidates on the ballot, which can benefit the electoral process.

On the other hand, there are also potential drawbacks to this approach. There is concern that the nomination process may lead to the selection of more extreme or fringe candidates by incentivizing them to focus on appealing to a small but passionate base of supporters rather than actively trying to appeal to a broader range of voters. Others argue this is already a problem in the current system, pointing to the behaviors of recently elected politicians. Another concern is that it may be more costly and time-consuming to administer a single, open primary, as this would involve more candidates and potentially more rounds of voting.

A single, open primary controlled by voters could give voters more control over elections and potentially more choices on the ballot. While this approach has other potential drawbacks, it could also lead to more diverse and representative candidates and a more democratic and responsive electoral process in the long run.

Expand Absentee Voting

Absentee voting, also known as the vote by mail, is a system that allows eligible voters to cast their ballots remotely without having to visit a polling place physically. People can do this by mail or other methods, such as online voting or voting at designated locations.

Absentee voting can be traced back to the Civil War when soldiers were granted the right to vote by mail. The system expanded over time to allow more voters to participate remotely, including those overseas, disabled, or unable to visit a polling place due to other circumstances.

Absentee voting can even give every American a choice to vote securely from the privacy, comfort, and safety of their home. Allowing voters to cast their ballots remotely can remove barriers to participation and make it easier for more people to participate in the electoral process. This capability can be particularly beneficial for those with difficulty physically attending a polling place, such as those with disabilities or living in rural areas.

There are also several potential drawbacks to absentee voting. One concern is the risk of fraud or errors, as handling and counting absentee ballots can be more complex than at polling places. Another concern is the potential for delays or issues with the mail, electronic or digital systems, which could affect the timely processing of ballots.

Absentee voting allows eligible voters to cast ballots remotely without visiting a polling place. It can give every American a choice to vote securely from the comfort and safety of home. However, we must carefully consider the risks and challenges that also come along with it.

Transform Election Funding

The Presidential Election Campaign Fund is a public financing program that provides funding for the presidential primary and general election campaigns of eligible candidates. It's part of the Federal Election Campaign Act of 1971, passed in response to concerns about the increasing cost of political campaigns, the potential for corruption, and the influence of special interests.

The United States funds the Presidential Election Campaign Fund through the checkoff system on individual income tax returns, allowing taxpayers to contribute a portion of their taxes voluntarily. The U.S. distributes these funds to eligible presidential candidates who agree to certain spending limits and disclosure requirements.

The primary purpose of the Presidential Election Campaign Fund is to reduce the influence of private money in the electoral process and promote a more level playing field for candidates. Public financing can help candidates run competitive campaigns without relying on large donations from special interests or wealthy individuals. It can also encourage more people to run for office, as it reduces the financial barriers to entry.

There are also some criticisms of the Presidential Election Campaign Fund. One issue is the U.S. funds it through the checkoff system, which has resulted in declining revenues in recent years. Another concern is that it hasn't always been effective in reducing the influence of private money in the electoral process, as some candidates have been able to raise significant amounts of money outside the system.

Running a political campaign is expensive for several reasons. One is that campaigns often require many resources to reach voters and communicate their message. These resources can include expenses such as advertising, staff salaries, travel, and campaign materials.

Another reason financing a campaign is challenging is that relatively few Americans can afford to donate to political campaigns. According to data from the Federal Election Commission, most campaign contributions come from a small number of wealthy donors. A small number of donations means that candidates must rely on a relatively small pool of funds to finance their campaigns, which can be costly.

This reliance on a small number of donors can make politicians dependent upon, and therefore responsive to, a tiny fraction of special-interest donors. These donors may have specific agendas or interests they want to advance, and candidates may feel pressure to support these agendas to secure their support. This pressure can lead to a situation in which politicians are more responsive to a small group of donors rather than the broader needs and interests of the general public.

One potential reform for the U.S. political campaign finance system is offering a small tax credit that voters could use to make a political donation with no out-of-pocket expense. Under this system, voters could claim a credit on their tax returns for a certain amount of money they contribute to a political campaign or organization. This reform would allow them to contribute without spending money, as the credit would offset the donation cost.

The government would only give eligibility for these credits to candidates and political groups that agree to fundraise solely from small donors. This small donor rule means they would not be able to accept donations from large donors or special interests but would have to rely on smaller contributions from individual voters. This rule could help reduce private money's influence in the electoral process and promote a more level playing field for candidates.

There are several potential benefits to this approach. One advantage is that it could increase the participation of small donors in the electoral process. By providing a tax credit for political contributions, the government might encourage more people to donate, as it wouldn't cost them any money out of pocket. Benefits could lead to a more representative and democratic political process, as more people would have a voice in the direction of campaigns and the issues emphasized.

There are also potential drawbacks to this approach. One concern is the cost of providing the tax credits, which could be significant depending on the number of people who choose to claim them. Another concern is the potential for abuse or fraud, as people might claim credit for donations fraudulently.

A small tax credit that voters can use to make a political donation with no out-of-pocket expense could increase the participation of small donors in the electoral process. While there are potential drawbacks, it could also help promote a more level playing field for candidates.

The system could potentially empower Political Action Committees (PACs) that only accept small donations from everyday people in several ways. This approach could level the PAC playing field as well.

Enact Reasonable Term Limits

Term limits refer to the maximum time an individual can serve in a political office. These limits can apply to various positions, such as members of Congress, state legislators, and even the President of the United States. The idea behind term limits is to prevent politicians from becoming entrenched in their positions and to encourage fresh ideas and perspectives.

One benefit of term limits is that they can help to prevent corruption. When politicians can remain in office for long periods, they may become more susceptible to influence from special interests and lobbyists. Imposing term limits forces politicians to leave office before they have the opportunity to become too entrenched in the system and potentially susceptible to corruption.

Term limits can also help to promote democratic ideals, such as fairness and equality. By limiting the time an individual can serve in a particular office, term limits also ensure that more people can participate in the political process. This term limitation can help create a more representative government that can better reflect the diverse perspectives and needs of the citizens it serves.

On the other hand, there are also drawbacks to term limits. One concern is that these limits might lead to a lack of institutional knowledge and experience. Forcing politicians to leave office after specific terms would ensure they take a lot of valuable knowledge and experience they have gained over the years. This drawback might also make it more difficult for new politicians to perform their duties effectively, leading to a lack of continuity in policy-making.

Another potential drawback of term limits is that they might give rise to career politicians who move from one office to another to maintain their political careers. This drawback could undermine the purpose of term limits and lead to a government with a small group of dominant politicians.

The debate over term limits is generally complex, with valid arguments. While term limits might potentially promote democratic ideals and prevent corruption, they can also lead to a lack of institutional knowledge and the rise of career politicians. We must carefully weigh the potential benefits and drawbacks before imposing term limits. A reasonable term limit for a particular office, similar to that of the President and Vice President, would need to be decided carefully and phased in over a fair amount of time.

Automatic Voter Registration

Using Automatic Voter Registration (AVR), we automatically register all eligible and interested voters when they interact with government agencies. This approach has the potential to significantly increase voter participation and make the electoral process more inclusive and democratic.

There are several reasons why AVR is desirable. First, AVR makes it easier for eligible voters to register to vote. Under traditional voter registration systems, individuals must take the initiative to seek out and complete a registration form, which can be a barrier to registration for some people. With AVR, however, eligible voters are automatically registered when interacting with government agencies, eliminating any need to take additional steps. This system can help ensure that more people can participate in the electoral process and have their voices heard.

Second, AVR can also increase the accuracy and completeness of voter registration rolls. Traditional voter registration systems can be prone to errors and inconsistencies, leading to the registration of ineligible voters or the omission of eligible voters from the rolls. AVR, on the other hand, uses government data to register eligible voters automatically. AVR can help reduce errors and ensure voter rolls are more accurate and up-to-date.

Third, AVR can also help reduce the risk of voter suppression and other forms of electoral fraud. By automating the voter registration process and using reliable data sources, AVR can help ensure that all eligible voters can participate in the electoral process and that the results of elections reflect the people's will. Voters could always opt out of being registered. Information could be transmitted electronically and securely to a central source maintained by the State.

Automatic Voter Registration is an important innovation of contemporary times that can increase voter participation, improve the accuracy and completeness of voter registration rolls, and reduce the risk of voter suppression and other forms of electoral fraud. By making it easier for eligible voters to register and participate in the electoral process, AVR can help ensure our democracy is more inclusive and representative of the people's will.

Lobbying and Lobbyist Bundling

There are several reasons it should be illegal for politicians to take money from lobbyists. Among them are just a few key considerations.

Conflicts of interest: When politicians take money from lobbyists, it creates a potential conflict of interest, as the politicians might feel obligated to prioritize their donors' interests over their constituents' interests. Conflicts of interest can lead to politicians making decisions that benefit the lobbyists and their clients rather than what's best for the public.

Corruption: The ability of lobbyists to make campaign contributions to politicians might also facilitate corruption, as it gives lobbyists a way to buy access and influence politicians. Contributions from lobbyists lead to politicians being more responsive to their donors' needs than their constituents and can undermine the integrity of the political process.

Undue influence: Allowing politicians to accept money from lobbyists also gives lobbyists disproportionate power in the political process. This allowance holds particularly true for special interest groups and corporate lobbyists, who often have deep pockets and can afford to make significant campaign contributions. Lobbyist contributions can create an imbalance of power between these groups and ordinary citizens. It can also make it more difficult for everyday people to have their voices heard in the political process.

Distraction from important issues: When politicians focus on fundraising and courting lobbyists, they may be less able to focus on the critical issues facing their constituents. Distraction can lead to a lack of attention to pressing problems and a failure to address the needs of ordinary people.

These are just a few compelling reasons why it should be illegal for politicians to take money from lobbyists. By eliminating this practice, we could help ensure that our political system is more transparent, accountable, representative, and responsive to the needs of the public rather than those of special interests.

Political campaigns are expensive, and politicians often rely on campaign donations to fund their efforts. Unfortunately, many politicians receive extraordinary sums of money through campaign donations from special interests who lobby them. They return the support by creating laws favorable to these special interests – even when those laws could hurt voters. This practice is known as "pay to play," and it's a serious problem in our political system.

For instance, politicians have created laws that give tax breaks to specific industries, even though these breaks have harmed the broader economy or led to budget deficits. They also have developed regulations that favored particular industries or created barriers to entry for new competitors. In some cases, politicians have even made laws that directly harmed the interests of their constituents, such as by having rolled back consumer protections or environmental regulations.

The problem of "pay to play" is made worse because many special interests can use their wealth and influence to shape the political process in their favor. They may hire lobbyists to advocate for their interests or donate to politicians who support their positions. This influence can give special interests an outsized effect on the political process and make it more difficult for ordinary people to have their voices heard by their elected representatives.

The practice of "pay to play" is a very serious problem in our political system today, and it's become one of the most compelling reasons why many people are disillusioned with politics and feel that their elected representatives aren't looking out for their interests. By reforming the campaign finance system and cracking down on the influence of special interests, we might help ensure that our political system is more transparent, accountable, and responsive to the needs of the public.

There is a solid argument to be made that people who get paid to lobby, in some cases known as "professional lobbyists," shouldn't be able to donate to politicians. This restriction is because allowing such donations can create a potential conflict of interest and undermine the political process's integrity.

There are several concrete examples of how lobbyists making campaign donations have created problems. In the United States, there have been numerous instances where politicians have passed laws to benefit their donors, even though those laws harmed the broader public. This knowledge has led to widespread cynicism and mistrust of the political process among the nation's voters, as many feel that their elected representatives are not looking out for their interests. This form of political lobbying undermines our democracy.

There are strong reasons to believe that people who get paid to lobby shouldn't be able to donate to politicians. By eliminating this practice, we can help ensure that our political system is more transparent, accountable, and responsive to the needs of the public rather than the interests of special interests.

Lobbyist bundling has become a practice in which lobbyists gather large campaign contributions from their friends and colleagues and then deliver them in one lump sum to politicians. This practice is highly controversial because it turns lobbyists into major fundraisers, incentivizing politicians to keep them happy by providing political favors.

Lobbyists can wield significant power and influence over politicians by serving as major fundraisers. This situation makes it more difficult for ordinary people to have their voices heard, as politicians are more responsive to large donors.

Lobbyist bundling also has the potential to facilitate corruption, as it gives lobbyists a way to buy access and influence politicians. This advantage can undermine the integrity of the political process and create the impression that politicians are more interested in serving their donors' interests than the public.

There are many reasons to ban lobbyist bundling. By eliminating this practice, we can help ensure that our political representatives serve the public's interests. It's essential to eliminate the possibility of undermining the integrity of our political process and ensure that politicians prioritize the interests of the public citizenry.

The Revolving Door Should Be Closed

Lobbyists and special interests routinely offer high-paying lobbying jobs to public officials to influence them while still in office. This practice is controversial because it can create a conflict of interest for politicians and undermine the political process's integrity.

Lobbyists and special interests offer high-paying lobbying jobs to public officials because they hope to gain access to and influence these officials. By providing lucrative employment opportunities after office, lobbyists and special interests can encourage politicians to prioritize their interests while in office and create a sense of indebtedness that may continue after the politicians leave office. It's not just lobbying jobs that are being offered either.

Typical forms of "after-office" employment also include memberships, corporate board-of-directors appointments, speakerships, college and university appointments, highly-paid speaking engagements, book publishing, consultancies, and other employee incentives. All can instill a sense of indebtedness while a politician's still in office.

Lobbyists and special interests also offer high-paying lobbying jobs to public officials because they know these officials have valuable, sometimes "inside" knowledge and connections that they can use to advance their interests. Politicians and their staffs often have extensive experience working within the government and may have valuable insights into the inner workings of the political system. By offering these individuals high-paying lobbying and other jobs after serving in political or other government service, lobbyists and special interests gain access to knowledge and use it to their political and other income-producing advantages.

Politicians and their staff often move straight from the government into lucrative lobbying jobs and other types of sponsored employment by lobbyists. They get paid to influence their former colleagues who remain in government. This practice is known as the "revolving door," and it's become a significant source of concern because, at minimum, it can create the impression that politicians are more interested in serving their future employers' interests than the public.

The practice of lobbyists and special interests offering high-paying lobbying jobs to public officials is controversial, as it can create conflicts of interest and undermine the integrity of the political process. We often refer to this practice as "influence peddling," too. By regulating this practice, we can help ensure our political system is more transparent, accountable, and responsive.

These are among many reasons for prohibiting elected representatives and senior staff from negotiating new jobs while still in office. Many believe they should be barred from paid lobbying for several years after leaving office. When politicians and their staff are allowed to negotiate new jobs while still in office, they might feel obligated and prioritize the interests of their future employers' interests over their constituents' interests. Their misplaced priority can lead to them making decisions that benefit their prospective employers rather than what's best for the public.

End Political Fundraising at Work

In the United States, elected representatives at all levels of government spend a significant amount of time fundraising. According to one Center for Responsive Politics study, the average member of Congress spends about one-third of their time on fundraising activities. This time amounts to about four hours per day or 20 hours per week.

There are several reasons why elected representatives spend so much time fundraising. One is that political campaigns are costly, and candidates must raise significant sums to run for office and get their message out to voters. The expense of campaigning means that politicians must devote considerable time to fundraising to secure the necessary resources to run their campaigns.

Another reason why elected representatives spend so much time fundraising is that they must constantly be on the lookout for new sources of campaign funding. This fundraising can be challenging and time-consuming, as politicians must build and maintain relationships with donors and comply with various campaign finance laws and regulations.

Elected representatives at the federal level are not the only ones who spend a significant amount of time fundraising. State and local officials also devote a substantial portion of their time to this activity, as they must also raise money to run their campaigns and support their agendas.

The average elected representative in the United States spends significant time fundraising. This activity can be challenging, time-consuming, and essential to the political process. It allows candidates to secure the resources they need to run their campaigns and advocate for their policies.

We have many reasons for barring politicians from fundraising during working hours or their typical workday. We base some of them on common sense.

If politicians can fundraise during normal days or working hours, it may detract from their ability to focus on their other duties and responsibilities. This distraction can lead to a lack of attention to important issues and a failure to address the needs of their constituents.

Allowing politicians to fundraise during working hours or their typical workday may create the perception that they use their official positions for personal gain. This assumption can undermine public trust in the political process and lead to widespread cynicism and mistrust of elected officials.

Fundraising can also create a potential conflict of interest for politicians. They may feel pressure to prioritize their donors' interests over their constituents. This pressure can lead to decisions that benefit donors rather than what's best for the public. It can also lead to a lack of attention to critical problems and a failure to address the needs of ordinary people.

We cited several reasons for barring politicians from fundraising during working hours or their typical workday, but there are many others. By eliminating this practice, we can help ensure that our political system is responsive to public interests.

Contributions in the Sunshine

Political campaign disclosure laws in the United States provide transparency and accountability in the political process. However, these laws are often outdated and broken. As a result, they fail to give citizens and journalists the information they need to follow the money trail in the political system.

One problem with current political campaign disclosure laws is that some contributions are never publicly available. This circumstance can make it difficult for citizens and journalists to track political money flow. Often, they must rely on paper filings and other manual processes to access this information.

Another problem with current political campaign disclosure laws is that they don't require real-time disclosure of donated political money. This absence of a timely disclosure means citizens and journalists must wait until after the fact to see who has donated money to a particular campaign. This delay can make it difficult to hold politicians accountable promptly. The public may not be aware of potential conflicts of interest or other problematic aspects of a campaign until it's too late.

There's a clear need for reform in this area, and one solution would be to require the disclosure of donated political money online and in real time. This rule would allow citizens and journalists to follow the money in the political system more timely and transparently. It would also help to ensure that politicians are held accountable for their fundraising activities.

Current political campaign disclosure laws are outdated and broken, and there's a clear need for reform. By requiring the disclosure of donated political money online and in real time, we could help ensure our political system is more transparent. This transparency might help prevent manipulation of the political process by politicians who use dark money and other sources to fund their political campaigns.

Political donors who hide behind secret-money groups can significantly impact elections, too, as these groups can spend money directly to influence elections. Individuals and organizations often make unlimited contributions to super PACs. These PACs use their funds to run ads to elect and defeat candidates. This lack of transparency by secret money groups can be a problem, making it difficult for voters to know who's behind the messages they see. It can also create the impression that hidden interests manipulate the political process.

There are several compelling reasons why stopping political donors from hiding behind secret-money groups is vital. One reason is that these groups often spend large sums of money to influence elections, giving them undue influence in the political process. Hidden donors make it more difficult for ordinary people to have their voices heard, as politicians may be more responsive to their donors.

Another reason it's essential to stop political donors from hiding behind secret-money groups is that it creates a sense of mistrust and cynicism among the public. When people don't know who is behind the messages they're seeing, they might be less likely to trust the political process and be less likely to participate in the democratic process.

It's vitally important to stop political donors from hiding behind secret-money groups to ensure that our political system is more transparent and accountable to the needs of the public. By requiring greater transparency in the political process, we can help ensure that our elections are fair and that politicians are accountable to the people they serve.'

Chapter 7

The Spirit of America

The Spirit of America is a concept that embodies the values, principles, and character of the United States of America. It's a unique blend of patriotism, pride, and optimism that's defined the American nation and its people for generations.

One of the most positive attributes of the Spirit of America is its emphasis on individual liberty and freedom. The Declaration of Independence and the Bill of Rights clearly state American these principles.

The U.S. has always been a beacon of hope and opportunity for people worldwide. People have come seeking to live their lives on their terms. The Spirit of America encourages them to think for themselves, speak their minds, and pursue their dreams without fear of oppression or persecution.

A positive attribute of the Spirit of America is its commitment to equality and justice. The United States was founded on the idea that everyone is created equal and deserves respect and dignity. The Spirit of America inspires Americans to stand for what is right, defend the vulnerable, and strive for a more just and fair society.

The U.S. people also characterize the Spirit of America as its spirit of innovation and progress. Americans have a long history of pushing the boundaries of what's possible and finding new and better ways to solve problems. America's spirit encourages people to be curious, question, and seek new knowledge and experiences.

The Spirit of America is defined by its spirit of community and compassion. Americans are known for their generosity and willingness to help others in need. Whether volunteering, donating to charity, or simply lending a helping hand, the Spirit of America inspires people to unite to make a difference in the world.

America's Spirit is a powerful force that defines the character of the United States and its people. It's a spirit of liberty, equality, innovation, and community that's shaped the nation and inspired generations of Americans to greatness

The American Dream: Citizenship and Inclusion

Citizenship in the United States has evolved significantly over time, and the struggles and victories of marginalized groups have played a central role in this evolution. At the country's founding, the government actively limited citizenship to white male property owners. However, various marginalized groups have fought for and achieved greater recognition and inclusion as full and equal citizens.

A significant milestone in U.S. citizenship was adopting the 14th Amendment to the Constitution in 1868. This amendment granted U.S. citizenship to all persons born or naturalized in the country. It extended certain legal protections to them too. The institution of slavery denied African-Americans citizenship and rights, but they actively achieved a significant victory by gaining these rights.

Another significant development in the history of U.S. citizenship was the adoption the 19th Amendment in 1920, which granted women the right to vote. This development was a substantial victory for the women's suffrage movement, which had been fighting for the right to vote for decades.

Over the years, other marginalized groups have also made significant strides in pursuing full and equal citizenship. For example, the civil rights movement of the 1950s and 1960s led to substantial advances in the rights of African-Americans, including eliminating segregation and expanding voting rights. More recently, the LGBTQ+ community has made significant progress in its quest for equal rights, including legalizing same-sex marriage in 2015.

The country needs to actively do more work to ensure that all citizens in the U.S. enjoy full and equal rights, even though these victories represent significant progress. Marginalized groups continue to face discrimination and barriers to full participation in society, and we must continue to work toward a more inclusive and just society for all.

Both struggles and victories have marked the evolution of U.S. citizenship, and the efforts of marginalized groups have played a central role in this process. By continuing to work toward greater equality and justice, we can build a more robust and inclusive democracy for all.

A Right to Vote: Suffrage in the Present Day

The history of voting rights in the United States is long and complex, marked by progress and setbacks. From the Republic's earliest days, the right to vote has been one of American politics' most fiercely contested issues.

Initially, the government restricted the right to vote to a narrow group of white male property owners. Over time, however, this exclusivity began to be challenged, and various groups began to fight for the expansion of voting.

One of the most significant battles for voting rights was the fight for women's suffrage. Women in the United States had been campaigning for the right to vote since the early 19th century. The 19th Amendment, ratified in 1920, finally granted women the right to vote. Figures such as Susan B. Anthony and Elizabeth Cady Stanton actively led the women's suffrage movement and worked tirelessly for decades to secure the right to vote.

Another significant milestone in voting rights was the Voting Rights Act of 1965, which aimed to end discriminatory voting practices that disenfranchised millions of African-Americans in the

South. The Act included provisions that prohibited states from imposing literacy tests and other discriminatory voting practices. It also provided active federal oversight of elections to ensure the rights of minority voters are protected.

Despite these significant advances, the struggle for voting rights in the United States is far from over. Ongoing efforts are still to expand access to the ballot and protect all voters' rights. In recent years, for example, there have been debates over voter identification laws, early voting, and the purging of voter rolls, all of which have implications for the right to vote.

The history of voting rights in the United States is a testament to the enduring struggle for democracy and the right to have a say in the decisions that affect our lives. History continues to be shaped by the efforts of those committed to expanding access to the ballot, ensuring that every vote counts.

Political Participation and the Role of Youth

Young people actively participate in politics, which is essential for maintaining the health and vitality of a democratic society. From the Republic's early days, young people have been at the forefront of political movements and have played a key role in shaping the nation's direction, even though, for the most part, young citizens have been denied equal rights and the extension of a voting privilege.

Young people can actively participate in politics in many ways other than by voting. At the same time, they await its qualified privilege until voting in the United States becomes an absolute right of citizenship for all citizens. Meanwhile, young people have the right to vote once they turn 18, and their participation in the electoral process is critical to the functioning of our form of a democratic society. Qualified voting young people actively shape this nation's future by casting their ballots and having a say in the decisions that shape the country.

Other young people without voting privilege can also actively participate in politics through social and political movements.

Throughout history, our nation's young citizens have been at the forefront of efforts to promote change and challenge injustice in this country. From the civil rights movement to the fight for LGBTQ+ rights, young people have been instrumental in advocating for the issues that matter to them and the nation.

Young people with qualified civic liberty, based on their age and other factors, actively participate in politics by holding public office. Many young adults have been elected to public office and have played a key role in shaping the policies and direction of this country. By serving in office, young adults often bring a fresh perspective and new ideas to the political process and help shape the nation's future.

Young people, especially young adults, have a long history of involvement in this nation's politics, and their participation has been essential to the health and vitality of our democratic society. By participating in elections, social and political movements, and public office, young people have had a say in the decisions that shaped the nation and helped shape the country's future. There's more work to be done and a rising tide of young voices demanding a more significant part in the political process, explicitly revising the 26th Amendment to lower the voting age in the United States.

The Struggle for Social Justice

Activism and social movements have shaped the nation's values and ideals. They've been instrumental in promoting positive change and challenging injustice. From the Republic's earliest days, ordinary people have come together to advocate for their beliefs and work towards a more just and fair society.

The civil rights movement is one of the most significant examples of activism and social movements in the United States. This movement, which spanned the 1950s and 1960s, was led by Martin Luther King Jr. and sought to end segregation and discrimination against African-Americans. Through protests, civil disobedience, and other forms of activism, the civil rights movement helped to bring about necessary changes, including the Civil Rights Act of 1964 and the Voting Rights Act of 1965.

Other examples of activism and social movements in the United States include the women's suffrage movement, which fought for the right to vote, and the LGBTQ+ rights movement, which has worked to promote equality and acceptance for people of all sexual orientations and gender identities.

Activism and social movements have shaped the nation's values and ideals. They've been instrumental in promoting positive change and challenging injustices. Through their efforts, ordinary people have made a difference and continue working towards a more just and fair society.

Civic Engagement and Responsible Citizenship

Citizens can get involved in their communities and make a difference in many ways. Individuals can choose the best approach that suits their skills, interests, and values.

Citizens can get more involved by participating in elections. By casting their ballots, citizens can have a say in the decisions that shape their communities and the nation. Still, volunteering is another way citizens can get involved by giving their time and talents. Whether it's helping out at a local school, working at a food bank, or participating in a beach clean-up, volunteering is a great way to make a difference and build connections with others.

Citizens can also get involved in their communities by advocating for the issues that matter to them. This advocacy can include writing letters to elected officials, participating in protests or rallies, or working with advocacy groups to promote change. Community service is another way citizens get involved and make a difference. By volunteering our time and talents to help others, citizens contribute to the common good and positively impact our communities.

We can get involved in our communities and make a difference in many other ways. We can choose the best approach that suits our skills, interests, and values. Many opportunities exist for citizen advocacy too. Whether through voting, volunteering, advocacy, or community service, all citizens can play an active role in shaping the direction of our communities and the nation.

American Spirit and the Power of Diversity

Diversity has long been one of the defining characteristics of the United States. It's played a central role in shaping the nation's character and identity. The United States is a nation of immigrants, and throughout its history, people from a wide range of cultural and ethnic backgrounds have come to this country seeking a better life.

One of the primary values of diversity in the United States is that it brings richness and depth to its culture. The United States is home to a wide range of artistic, culinary, and musical traditions, and the diversity of these traditions has helped to create a vibrant and dynamic cultural landscape. In addition, the diversity of the United States has contributed to its scientific and technological achievements, as people from different cultural backgrounds have brought their unique perspectives and approaches to problem-solving.

Another value of diversity in the United States is that it promotes social and political harmony. By bringing people from different backgrounds together, diversity helps to build understanding and respect between other groups. It also helps foster a sense of unity and shared purpose as people from different cultures and experiences work toward common goals.

Diversity is a source of strength and resilience. By embracing diversity, the U.S. draws upon a wide range of skills, talents, and perspectives, which has helped the nation to adapt and thrive in the face of changing circumstances.

Diversity is also valued in the United States and has contributed in countless ways to its character and identity. By embracing and valuing diversity, the United States has created a rich and dynamic culture, promoted social and political harmony, and built resilience and strength.

The Protection of Individual Rights

The Constitution of the United States is the supreme law of the land, and it plays a vital role in safeguarding the rights and freedoms of Americans. The Constitution is a document that establishes the framework of the government and sets out the basic principles and values that guide the nation.

One of the ways the Constitution protects Americans' rights is through the Bill of Rights, the first ten amendments to the Constitution. The Bill of Rights guarantees various fundamental rights and freedoms, including freedom of speech, religion, and the press, the right to bear arms, and a fair and speedy trial. These rights are essential to the functioning of a democratic society. They form the foundation of the liberties that Americans enjoy.

The Bill of Rights and the U.S. Constitution include provisions protecting the right to vote. Once again, it's important to cite the distinction between the definition and context of the word "right" as used in that former statement. The 15th Amendment also prohibits states from denying the right to vote based on race, color, or previous condition of servitude. The 19th Amendment guarantees women the right to vote, the 24th Amendment prohibits using poll taxes and other discriminatory voting practices, and the 26th Amendment extends the right to vote to citizens over 18. Still, the right to vote for elected representation in the U.S. Congress or federal government is not a "right" currently being extended to all U.S. citizens. Tens of millions of U.S. citizens are presently excluded from voting in the United States.

The Constitution continues to serve as a beacon of hope and liberty for people worldwide. The U.S. Constitution is the country's fundamental document guaranteeing all Americans' protections, rights, and freedoms.

American Spirit and the Importance of Education

Education is an essential component of a healthy and democratic society. It plays a vital role in fostering a well-informed and engaged citizenry. By providing individuals with the knowledge and skills they need to understand and participate in civic life, education helps to create an informed and active citizenry capable of shaping the nation's direction.

One of the primary ways education promotes civic engagement is by teaching students about the nation's history, values, and principles. Through their education, students learn about the founding of the United States, the Constitution, and the principles of democracy. They also learn about the struggles and achievements of different groups and the role ordinary people have played in shaping the nation. By actively understanding these things, students can engage with the day's issues and make informed decisions about the nation's future.

Another way education fosters a well-informed and engaged citizenry is by teaching students critical thinking and problem-solving skills. These skills are essential for understanding complex issues and solving the nation's challenges. By teaching students to think critically and to analyze information, schools help to prepare young people to be active and responsible citizens.

Education is crucial in preparing young people for their roles as citizens by teaching them the values and habits of good citizenship. Citizenship education teaches students the importance of volunteering, community service, and political participation. By instilling these values in young people, schools help to create a new generation of engaged and responsible citizens.

Education is vital to a healthy and democratic society. Through education, students learn about the nation's history, values, and principles, develop critical thinking and problem-solving skills, and learn the values and habits of good citizenship. These are all essential for preparing young people for their roles as responsible and active citizens.

Political Parties and the American Government

Political parties play a central role in the political landscape of the United States. Parties shape the policy debates that shape the nation. Political parties are organizations that unite people with similar political beliefs and goals. They work to promote their agendas and to win elections.

The Democratic Party and the Republican Party are the two major political parties in the U.S. These parties have a long history in the nation, and they've played a central role in shaping the nation's political landscape.

Political parties serve several essential functions in the American political system. First and foremost, they provide a way for people with similar political beliefs to come together and work toward common goals. Parties help unite like-minded people and provide a way for people to work toward their shared objectives.

Parties also play a role in shaping the policy debates that shape the nation. Parties work to promote their agendas and influence the policy decisions made by the government. They do this by fielding candidates for office, campaigning for their candidates, and advocating for their policies.

Finally, political parties help to organize and structure the political process. They provide a way for people to get involved in politics and have a say in the nation's decisions. Through their participation in political parties, people can work to shape the direction of the country and make a difference in their communities.

American Spirit and the Global Community

The United States has always been a significant player on the global stage, and its actions and policies have substantially impacted international events. As a world leader, the United States has many responsibilities and obligations to the rest of the world. It's had a unique role to play in shaping the course of global events too.

One of the primary ways the United States has interacted with the rest of the world is through its foreign policy. The U.S. has a long history of engaging with other countries to promote its interests and advance its values. U.S. foreign policy has included efforts to promote democracy and human rights, combat terrorism and other global threats, and address climate change and international economic development.

Historically, the U.S. has also interacted with the rest of the world through its military and economic power. The U.S. actively uses its large and powerful military to defend the nation and its global interests. In addition, the U.S. has a strong and influential economy. This interaction between military defense and its economic power has helped the U.S. play a leading role in shaping the global financial system.

As a global leader, the United States has some responsibilities and obligations to the rest of the world. These include maintaining peace and stability, promoting democracy and human rights, and addressing global challenges such as poverty, disease, and environmental degradation. To fulfill these responsibilities, the United States must work closely with other countries and international organizations and be willing to cooperate and compromise to find solutions to global problems.

The United States has a significant impact on global events and plays a major role in shaping the course of world affairs. As a global leader, the U.S. has many responsibilities and obligations to the rest of the world. It must work to maintain peace, promote democracy and human rights, and address global challenges.

The Spirit of America is a powerful force that defines the character of the United States and its people. A spirit of liberty, equality, innovation, and community has shaped the nation and inspired generations of Americans to greatness.

Chapter 8

A New Quest for Suffrage

The right to vote is considered a fundamental privilege of citizenship in the United States. However, laws actively exclude many citizens from exercising their right to vote in federal, state, and local elections, leading to many controversies. These exclusions have had significant consequences for both the individuals involved and the country's political landscape.

In a representative democracy, a vote is a crucial tool for citizens to have a say in the decisions that affect their lives. It allows people to choose representatives and hold them accountable for their actions. Voting is a fundamental privilege extended to U.S. citizens and protected by law. While voting is essential to the functioning of a democratic society, in the United States, much work must still be done to ensure equal access and to make the privilege a genuine right.

A right to vote is essential for individual citizens and the health and stability of a representative democratic system. People can hold their elected representatives accountable for their actions when they can vote. The exclusion of many of the nation's citizenry from voting is not a truly representative democracy. The voting right of individual citizens helps ensure that government is responsive to the needs and concerns of its citizens. Still, without the universal right to vote in the U.S., millions of citizens have no voice in our democracy. Each citizen, whether an adult or child, represents a crucial part of our U.S. community, of our nation.

Allowing a few citizens to represent the voices and interests of all is not a democracy unless all select those few voices to represent them. Suppose it must be that adult parents speak as the voices of their U.S. citizen children through proxy voting or some other system of guardianship representation. In that case, doing so will ensure a more representative government in this country, responsive to the will of a more significant number of our U.S. citizens.

As we evolve as a democratic republic utilizing a representative form of democracy, many believe we must enable all U.S. citizens to vote. We have no further to look than through history to learn what happens if we don't. Systems rife with partisan division and corruption, such as ours, have historically evolved into autocratic dictatorships and empires.

Meanwhile, enabling a voting system for all citizens isn't far-fetched or impractical. Just as today, many disabled Americans are accommodated in voting, so too many believe children might be. Central to the logic of this argument is that if a child U.S. citizen is old enough to accomplish the act and expresses a desire to do so, as a U.S. citizen, their fundamental right of citizenship in our democracy should not be denied.

In addition to holding elected officials accountable, the vote allows citizens to have a say in the policy decisions shaping their communities and country. It gives people a voice in the political process and will enable them to have a stake in their society's direction. If the nation's future doesn't belong to its nation's citizen children, who does it belong to?

A vote is also essential for promoting diversity and inclusion in the political process. By allowing all citizens to participate in the electoral process, regardless of their background, representative democracy can ensure that the voices and perspectives of a wide range of people are heard and considered. During this country's ugliest past, this government has used many tactics to deny the people's voice by denying them access to the vote. Among these tactics were intelligence and social maturity tests, an extreme system of qualification as a means of exclusion from voting. How is it different when these same tactics are argued as applicable to this nation's citizen children? Again, many believe a family of two U.S. citizen parents with six U.S. citizen children under age 18 should be extended eight votes, not just two, if the U.S. were indeed a representative democracy.

The right to vote is not always secure. Various factors, such as voter suppression, gerrymandering, and other forms of interference, have threatened the right to vote. A democratic society must protect and defend the right to vote and ensure all citizens have equal access to the ballot box.

Many believe we must also soon consider the plight of millions of U.S. citizens residing in the U.S. Virgin Islands, Puerto Rico, Guam, the Marianna Islands, and other of America's insular territories regarding their voting rights and representation in the U.S. Congress. It's unjust to allow one of the three central bodies of our government to rule these citizens with absolute plenary authority, establishing a literal authoritarian dictatorship over millions of U.S. citizens. Doing so, virtually denying them a voice in the decisions that affect their lives and those of their U.S. citizen children, is unjust and undemocratic. Yet, this is the U.S. Congress's current role in these millions of U.S. citizens' lives.

Many also believe full voting rights and perhaps even statehood should be extended to the District of Columbia's citizens. Like millions of others, they too have been excluded from true representation in Congress, and consequently from the total and fundamental rights of U.S. citizenship, by not being allowed to participate entirely and fully contribute their voices to our democracy.

Counting Heads

The 2020 Census estimates that approximately 331 million people actively reside in the 50 states of the United States as of 2021 (2020, Census.) This estimate includes U.S. citizens and non-citizens. The U.S. Census Bureau conducts a decennial census to count the

United States resident population, including all people who live in the 50 states, the District of Columbia, and Puerto Rico. The most recent census, conducted in 2020, counted a resident U.S. citizen population of 331 million. Approximately 328 million lived in the 50 states and the District of Columbia, while around 3 million lived in Puerto Rico.

It's difficult to accurately estimate the number of documented immigrants living in the 50 states of the United States. According to the U.S. Census Bureau, in 2019, approximately 44 million foreign-born people lived in the United States, comprising about 13% of the total U.S. population. About 27 million were naturalized U.S. citizens, while approximately 17 million were non-citizens. How many foreign-born people lived in the 50 states instead of Puerto Rico or other U.S. territories is unclear. Most recent Census data indicate that approximately 311 million birthright and naturalized U.S. citizens live in the 50 states and Washington D.C.

As of 2021, approximately 4 million U.S. citizens live in the insular territories of the United States. The insular territories are politically affiliated with the U.S. but aren't a part of the United States, as would strictly be defined as the States of the United States. These territories are the U.S. Virgin Islands, Puerto Rico, Guam, American Samoa, the Northern Mariana Islands, and other minor outlying islands. Most U.S. citizens living in the insular territories reside in Puerto Rico, with a population of approximately 3.2 million. The U.S. Virgin Islands, Guam, and American Samoa also have significant populations of U.S. citizens.

It's important to note that the insular territories have a unique status within the United States. While the residents of these regions are U.S. citizens, they don't have the exact political representation as citizens in the states. The Office of Insular Affairs within the U.S. Department of the Interior administers them, and they have limited self-governance.

Also important to note is that the term "documented immigrant" refers to a person living in the United States with legal immigration status. This documentation status includes people who have obtained visas, green cards, or other forms of authorized stay. It doesn't include people living in the U.S. without legal permission. It's impossible to accurately estimate the number of undocumented immigrants living in the 50 states, as official population counts don't capture these individuals.

Accurate population and citizenship numbers are difficult to state precisely. Approximately 311 million U.S. citizens reside in the 50 states and the federal District of Columbia or Washington D.C. This number doesn't include any estimated number of non-citizen or undocumented immigrants. Approximately 4 million U.S. citizens also reside in the 16 insular territories.

It's even harder to estimate the number of U.S. citizens living abroad. According to the U.S. Department of State, approximately 9 million U.S. citizens living overseas, including military personnel, dependents, and civilian employees of the U.S. government. However, this number doesn't include U.S. citizens living abroad independently, for private purposes, or for secret governmental reasons. This figure does not account for many other U.S. citizens living abroad.

The U.S. Census Bureau also tracks data on the foreign-born population living in the United States, which includes naturalized U.S. citizens. According to the Census Bureau, in 2019, approximately 44 million foreign-born people lived in the United States, comprising about 13% of the total U.S. population. It's unclear how many foreign-born U.S. citizens are living abroad.

It's also difficult to accurately estimate the number of registered voters in the United States because voter registration rules vary from state to state. In some states, voting is restricted to registered voters, while in others, citizens can register to vote on the day of the election.

According to the U.S. Census Bureau, in 2020, there were approximately 246 million people of voting age (18 years or older) in the United States. However, not all of these people are registered to vote. The U.S. Elections Project (2021, Project), which tracks voter participation in the United States, estimates that as of October 2021, approximately 164 million people were registered to vote in the U.S. This represents about two-thirds of the voting-age population.

It's also important to note that the number of registered voters changes over time as people move, become ineligible to vote (e.g., due to incarceration or loss of citizenship), or pass away. The U.S. Elections Project estimates that the number of registered voters in the United States has steadily increased over the past few decades due to efforts to improve voter registration and participation.

According to the United States Census Bureau, as of July 1, 2020, an estimated 705,749 people were living in Washington, D.C. This estimate is based on the most recent data from the Census Bureau's population clock. Please remember that this number is an estimate and may not be the most up-to-date information.

It's challenging to determine how many children live in Washington, D.C., as the United States Census Bureau doesn't regularly release information on the number of children living in specific geographical areas. According to data from the American Community Survey (ACS), in 2019 (ACS, 2019), approximately 29% of the population of Washington, D.C., was under 18. This number would equate to about 204,515 children living in the district, based on the most recent population estimate of 705,749 people. Again, please remember that these numbers are estimates and may not be the most up-to-date information.

According to the United States Census Bureau, as of July 1, 2020, an estimated 2,195,541 U.S. citizens over 18 live in Puerto Rico. This estimate is the most recent data from the Census Bureau's population clock. This number represents U.S. citizen adults only.

Exactly how many children live in Puerto Rico is estimated, as the United States Census Bureau doesn't regularly release information on the number of children living in specific geographical areas. According to data from the American Community Survey, as of 2019, approximately 30.5% of Puerto Rico's population was under 18. This number would equate to about 668,523 children living in the territory, based on the most recent population estimate of 2,195,541 people. Again, please remember that these numbers are estimates and may not be up-to-date or representative of U.S. citizenry information. The difference between the combined data of the Census and ACS may be accounted for by the collection of data representing the number of U.S. Citizens residing there.

Determining the exact number of adult citizens who live in the United States' insular territories isn't possible, as the United States Census Bureau doesn't regularly release this information. However, according to data from the U.S. Census Bureau, as of July 1, 2020, the estimated populations of the four inhabited insular territories of the United States (excluding Puerto Rico) are American Samoa: 54,382; Guam: 167,294; Northern Mariana Islands: 53,883; U.S. Virgin Islands: 106,405, or a total U.S. citizenry of 381,964.

According to data from the American Community Survey, as of 2019, the estimated percentages of the populations of the four inhabited insular territories that are under the age of 18 are American Samoa: 32.1%, Guam: 32.7%, Northern Mariana Islands: 36.9% and U.S. Virgin Islands: 33.1%.

Using these percentages and the most recent population estimates from the U.S. Census Bureau, we can estimate the number of children living in each of the insular territories as American Samoa: 17,569, Guam: 55,276, Northern Mariana Islands: 19,938, and U.S. Virgin Islands: 35,397, or a total number of U.S. citizen children as 128,180. Please remember that these numbers are estimates and may not be the most up-to-date information.

A review of the data poses some troubling facts. One is that of the 311 million citizens in the 50 United States and Puerto Rico, and of the 264 million U.S. citizens eligible to vote, only about 164 million are registered. This number means approximately 100 million eligible and qualified U.S. citizens don't vote.

To put this number into perspective, the results of the past three presidential elections in terms of the difference between the number of votes received by the winning candidate and the number of votes received by the runner-up were, in the 2020 election: Joe Biden won with a margin of 7,051,141 votes over Donald Trump; in the 2016 election: Donald Trump won with a margin of 77,744 votes over Hillary Clinton, and; in the 2012 election: Barack Obama won with a margin of 3,974,586 votes over Mitt Romney. Those missing 100 million votes would have significantly impacted all these elections. Maybe the results would have been the same, and perhaps not. Still, it's interesting to ponder this possibility, along with the one that would have been determined if all citizens, and not just those 100 million plus unregistered to vote, had voted.

The United States Elections Project, a comprehensive database of electoral data maintained by Dr. Michael McDonald, an Associate Professor at the University of Florida, sourced the results of the past three presidential elections. The database contains official election results from all 50 states and the District of Columbia and is updated regularly to reflect the most current and accurate information available.

It's important to note that these numbers represent the total votes each candidate receives nationwide. They don't consider the electoral college or other factors influencing the election's outcome.

There are 164 million registered voters in the U.S., 50 states, and D.C., the latter voting only for the distribution of its three electors in the electoral college, for the presidency and vice-presidency in the federal general election. This number is 164 million voters of an eligible adult population of 264 million. Extending voting rights to all 311 million citizens residing in the U.S. 50 states and D.C., regardless of age or criminal history, would profoundly impact the landscape of American politics and the U.S. Government. Further, this would likely dilute the possibility of influential political corruption in our democracy and reduce significant political partisanship control of any branch of our federal government.

The 2020 Census pegs the number of birthright and naturalized citizens residing in the U.S. 50 and D.C. at 311 million. Extending suffrage to 'adult' citizens of Puerto Rico would add approximately 2,195,541 voters, or extending to all Puerto Rican citizens, including 668,523 'children,' would result in 2,864,064 new eligible voters. Respectively, extending suffrage to adult U.S. citizens residing in the U.S. insular territories would add 309,119 new U.S. adult voters. Including their 128,180 children, the total number of new voters added would be 381,964.

Extending the right to vote to all U.S. citizens residing in Puerto Rico and the insular territories would add approximately 3.5 million, new voters. So, if voting were to be extended to all U.S. citizens, regardless of their geographic location, age, or criminal history, there would be a tremendous shift in politics and government in the United States.

Considering the number of individuals denied U.S. voting regardless of their having U.S. citizenship status, and also considering the low voter turnout among eligible citizens, it becomes immediately apparent that voter participation in the United States doesn't accurately represent it as either a "representative democracy" or a "representative republic." For this reason, the current U.S. form of representative democracy also doesn't accurately reflect a majority population influence in U.S. government selection, or a government of the people, by the people.

The Dream of True Universal Suffrage

One controversial group of citizens excluded by law from voting law are those convicted of felonies. Voting rights aren't the only "rights" controversy concerning this group of citizens since the 13th Amendment also excludes them from protections barring the condition of involuntary servitude, effectively continuing its practice in the United States among its citizenry for the past 168 years, as of this book's publication. In many states, people with felony convictions aren't allowed to vote, even after they've completed their sentences. This exclusion can significantly impact these individuals, making it more difficult to fully reintegrate into society and limiting their ability to participate in the political process.

There are several ways convicted criminals can restore their voting rights, depending on the state where they reside. Individuals with felonies can regain the right to vote through voting rights restoration. This process varies by state but generally involves petitioning the government to restore their right to vote. In some states, this process can be automatic once an individual has completed their sentence, while in others, it may require a hearing or other legal proceedings.

Another way that individuals can regain their voting rights is through executive clemency. This method is a form of executive action that allows the governor of a state to restore an individual's voting rights. Individuals with good conduct and a desire to reintegrate into society generally receive executive clemency. Still, it's rare since politicians are often held to public scrutiny by their opponents regarding how they treat criminals. They are often accused of "being soft on crime" when providing even the most modest concession to those convicted.

Some states have adopted laws that automatically restore voting rights to individuals with felonies once they've completed their sentences. Examples of these states include Vermont, Maine, and California. These laws actively grant the right to vote to individuals who have served their time and paid their debt to society. These States recognize that individuals should not be permanently denied the privilege of voting.

As previously discussed, another group of citizens excluded from voting are those who are under the age of 18. While young people may be interested in participating in the political process, they're not allowed to vote in federal elections until they reach the age of 18. This exclusion can limit the ability of young people to have a say in the decisions that affect their lives. It can also limit the diversity of perspectives represented in the political process.

Voices of the Future

Imagine a country where U.S. citizen children under 18 have the right to vote. This idea may seem radical, but it's not without precedent. In some countries, such as Austria and Brazil, the voting age is as low as 16. And there's already a growing movement in the U.S. to lower the voting age to 16 or perhaps even 15.

Expanding the right to vote to young people under 18 could have an enormous impact on the political landscape of the United

States by potentially improving how the country is run and the quality of the candidates elected. It would give young people a more significant say in the decisions that affect their lives and would recognize their citizenship and the contributions they make to society.

Aside from those mentioned, many other arguments favor expanding the right to vote to children under 18. One view is that young people are impacted by political decisions just as much as adults and should have a say. For example, young people are affected by education, the environment, and gun control. Allowing them to vote would give them a more significant stake in the political process and could encourage greater civic engagement.

Another argument is that young people are more likely to be politically active and engaged when they have the right to vote. Studies have shown that young people allowed to vote are more likely to participate in political activities such as volunteering, campaigning, and discussing politics with their peers. This increased engagement could lead to a more informed and engaged electorate overall.

Children are affected by political decisions made by adults, as these decisions can majorly impact their lives and prospects. This impact is particularly true regarding education funding, healthcare policy, and environmental regulations, which can profoundly influence children's well-being and opportunities.

One of the most glaring ways children are affected by political decisions is through education funding. The amount of money allocated to schools and educational programs can significantly impact the quality of education children receive. For example, schools with inadequate funding may be unable to afford new textbooks or technology, which can hinder students' learning. Similarly, cuts to education funding can lead to larger class sizes, making it more difficult for students to receive the individualized attention they need to succeed.

Healthcare policy is another area where children are affected by political decisions. Access to healthcare is critical for children's physical and mental health. Policies that limit access to healthcare can have severe consequences for children. For example, children who don't have access to preventive care or timely treatment for illnesses may experience more severe health problems, which can have long-term consequences for their overall health and well-being throughout their lifetimes.

Children are also affected by political decisions related to environmental regulations. Young people are particularly vulnerable to the adverse effects of pollution and ecological degradation. Their bodies are still developing into adolescence and adulthood, making them more susceptible to the harmful effects of toxins and other toxic substances. Therefore, political decisions related to environmental regulations can significantly impact children's health and prospects.

Young people have the right to free expression and free assembly, fundamental rights protected by the 1st Amendment. Extending the right to vote to children would allow them to exercise these rights fully.

Young people are capable of understanding the political process and making informed decisions. Many children learn about government and politics in school. Some may even actively participate in mock elections or debate clubs.

Allowing U.S. citizen children to vote could increase youth participation in the political process. Extension of voting rights could result in a more representative government that's also more responsive to the needs and concerns of younger citizens, not just those of adults.

Children are the future of U.S. society. Their voices and perspectives should be heard and considered in the decision-making process. There are many reasons why this is important.

Children will inherit the world we leave behind and lead our society in its future. They will be responsible for shaping the direction of our communities, country, and world. Therefore, they must develop the skills, knowledge, and perspective necessary to be effective leaders as soon as possible. By listening to children's voices and considering their views, we can help to foster a new generation of leaders who are more in touch with the needs and concerns of the people they serve than were past generations.

It's equally important to note that children bring a unique and valuable perspective to decision-making. Children are often more open-minded and receptive to new ideas and can add fresh perspectives to problems and challenges. By listening to children's voices and considering their views, we can benefit from their fresh perspectives and develop more innovative and practical solutions to our problems. By giving children a seat at the table, we can help to shape a better future for all of us.

Some children can already participate in civic activities, such as volunteering and community service. Extending the right to vote would let them take an even more active role in their communities. They also can bring fresh ideas to the political process, which could lead to more innovative and effective policies.

Extending children the political privilege to vote would help promote a culture of civic engagement and responsibility at a young age. Children voting could also lead to a more representative and diverse government, as U.S. children come from various socioeconomic and cultural backgrounds, just like adults. Many countries worldwide allow a child to vote in local or national elections, and there is no reason why the United States should not do the same.

There will be some challenges in expanding the right to vote to children under 18. Some may persist in the argument that young people aren't mature enough or don't have enough life experience to make informed decisions at the ballot box. The major political parties will likely continue to object, as a larger, less controllable electorate is a threatening prospect for them. Others may be concerned about the potential for underage voters to be influenced or manipulated by outside interests.

During the Civil Rights Movement, the nation adopted the 14th Amendment and other measures, such as the Civil Rights Act of 1964 and the Voting Rights Act of 1965, to eliminate Jim Crow laws and literacy tests as qualifications for voting. These Acts effectively granted all adult citizens, with some qualified exceptions, the right to vote.

It's fair to note that in the United States, mentally disabled individuals have the right to vote and are protected from discrimination by the Americans with Disabilities Act (ADA). The ADA prohibits discrimination against individuals with disabilities, including mental impairments, in various areas, including voting. We've actively barred literacy testing and arbitrary assessments of one's life experiences as they are inequitable by law. Many argue these laws must now also be applied to the nation's children under 18,

As to being influenced or manipulated by outside interests, it's argued that young people are no more vulnerable than adults who are already granted the right. Adults, too, are influenced by all sorts of things affecting how they vote. In point of fact and in terms of maturity, anyone who's witnessed some adult behaviors in and around polling places on election day can undoubtedly attest that young people could be no less behaviorally mature than them.

If one considers it carefully, individual U.S. citizen children pay state and federal taxes on many types of income. Some children also work and pay taxes, so they contribute taxes without representation when denied the vote. Many times today, U.S. citizen children are being tried as adults in the U.S. Courts. It's arbitrary to hold them to these adult standards while denying them the full privileges of their U.S. citizenship. Finally, it would seem reasonable they are afforded a voice in the future of U.S. policy since those policies affect their futures in this great nation.

Implementing education and voter outreach programs can overcome many challenges as the nation transitions to a more inclusive electorate. By giving young people the tools and resources they'll need to make informed decisions, we can help ensure their votes are meaningful and impactful.

Expanding the right to vote to children under 18 can potentially change the political landscape of the United States vastly. It would give young people a more significant say in the decisions that affect their lives and could lead to greater civic engagement and a more informed and engaged electorate. It's likely extending suffrage to children wouldn't be popular in Congress, so it will probably be necessary first to seek its mandate in the Supreme Court, arguing for enforcement of existing Constitutional Amendments and federal laws.

Granting children under 18 the right to vote would necessitate adjustments to the voting process. Some potential changes might include areas like voter registration. Creating new forms and procedures is necessary to include young people under 18 in the voter registration processes.

There might be a need to provide more education about the voting process and the importance of civic engagement to children to ensure they're informed and prepared to participate in elections. Polling places might need to be adjusted to accommodate children by providing separate areas for minors to cast their ballots or having special hours for children to vote. Ballots might need to be revised to include issues and candidates more relevant to children to ensure they have the information they need to make informed decisions. To progressively accommodate children in the voting process, it might be necessary to phase in the implementation of these changes.

For example, we could gradually roll out voter registration for minors, starting with children who are 16 or 17 years old and expanding to include younger children over time. Similarly, we could provide additional education and resources to help children understand the voting process and the issues at stake in elections. By gradually introducing these changes, it may be possible to ensure that children can fully and effectively participate in the democratic process.

Another group of U.S. citizens excluded from voting by law are adults residing in the 16 insular territories. Imagine the political landscape where residents of the U.S. insular territories, such as Puerto Rico, the U.S. Virgin Islands, Guam, and other territorial citizens, have the right to vote in U.S. presidential elections. This scenario might seem far-fetched, but it's not impossible to envision.

Millions of U.S. citizens residing in the United States insular islands, including Puerto Rico, Guam, the Virgin Islands, and American Samoa, are denied the right to vote in federal elections. This grave injustice has far-reaching consequences for the residents of these islands, and many believe it's time for the U.S. to grant them the right to vote.

Ensuring full representation of citizens residing in the insular islands in the U.S. government is a compelling reason to grant them the right to vote. Currently, the residents of these islands don't have voting representatives in Congress, meaning they have no say in the decisions that affect their lives and communities. This lack of representation is fundamentally unfair, as all U.S. citizens should have the right to have their voices heard and their interests represented in government.

Arguments supporting their voting and consequential representation exclusion from Congress mostly center around the issue of federal taxation and that the island's residents don't pay a proportionate tax share. There are at least two flaws in taking this position. Washington D.C.'s population pays federal tax and doesn't have representation in Congress either. Two poses the question of equity. Is it equitable to hold voting rights hostage to the economy? Is it fair to charge, in the form of taxes, for the fundamental privilege of citizenship – the right to vote? In other words, is the most basic privilege of U.S. citizenship for sale?

Another reason to grant the insular islands the right to vote is that it would help to promote democracy and civic engagement in these communities. Since voting is a fundamental right and an essential aspect of civic participation, granting the right to vote to the residents of these islands would encourage them to become more involved in the political process and take a more active role in shaping their communities and their country.

Finally, granting the insular islands the right to vote would be a powerful symbol of the United States' commitment to equal treatment and justice for all its citizens. It would demonstrate that the U.S. values the contributions and perspectives of all its citizens, regardless of where they live.

Many compelling arguments exist for granting the U.S. insular territories the right to vote. Creating a more inclusive and just society for all can be achieved by giving these citizens the right to vote, which ensures their full representation in the U.S. government, promotes democracy and civic engagement, and demonstrates our commitment to equal treatment.

There are several ways to expand the right to vote in insular territories. One option would be for Congress to pass legislation granting voting rights to the residents of the U.S. territories. Another option would be for the U.S. Supreme Court to rule that the right to vote is a fundamental right that extends to all U.S. citizens, regardless of where they live.

While there might be some challenges to expanding the right to vote to the insular territories, the benefits would be significant. Ensuring all U.S. citizens' voices are heard and making the political system more representative of the whole would help improve the political system. It would also be a step toward greater equality and justice for the residents of the U.S. territories, who have long been denied full political representation despite being U.S. citizens.

Inclusion of all currently excluded groups could expand the representative democracy and republic. It could also change the country's political direction for the better. For instance, allowing people with felony convictions to vote could help to reduce recidivism and promote rehabilitation, as these individuals would have a more significant stake in the political process.

The history of controversies surrounding the right to vote in the United States highlights the importance of ensuring that all citizens can participate in the political process. Expanding voting rights to all U.S. citizens would help elections be more representative of the population of the United States of America.

Representative Democracy

Representative democracy is a form of government in which citizens elect representatives to make decisions. At its best, representative democracy embodies equality, justice, and participation ideals.

Among the ideals of representative democracy is equality. All citizens, regardless of their background or circumstances, should have an equal say in the decisions that affect their lives. True equality means that every citizen should have an equal opportunity to participate in the political process by voting, running for office, or voicing their opinions and concerns.

Another tenet of representative democracy is justice. Representatives should be accountable to the citizens they serve and make fair and just decisions for all. To ensure equal justice, representatives should act impartially and consider the needs and interests of all community members rather than being influenced by special interests or personal gain.

Finally, participation is an essential ideal of representative democracy. All citizens should be able to engage with the political process and have a say in the decisions that affect their lives. Freedom of participation means citizens should be able to freely express their opinions, engage in public debate, and hold their representatives accountable for their actions.

Representative democracy in the United States has evolved since the country's founding in the late 18th century. At its inception, the U.S. was predominantly agricultural, and the right to vote was generally limited to white male property owners. Over time, however, the franchise has been expanded to include a wider group of citizens.

A significant milestone in the evolution of representative democracy in the U.S. was the adoption of the Constitution in 1787, which established a federal government with a system of checks and balances to help ensure that no one branch of government became too powerful. The Constitution contained provisions for the election of representatives to the federal government, including the U.S. Congress and the presidency.

Another significant development in the history of representative democracy in the U.S. was the adoption the 19th Amendment in 1920, which granted women the right to vote. This development was a milestone in the women's suffrage movement, which had sought the right to vote for decades.

Over the years, other groups have also gained the right to vote, including African-Americans, Native Americans, and individuals 18 and older. The Constitution of the U.S. protects the right to vote today, and it is generally extended to qualified citizens, regardless of race, gender, or other factors.

Despite these advances, pursuing representative democracy in the U.S. is challenging. Some individuals and groups still face barriers to full participation in the political process, including voter suppression, gerrymandering, or discrimination inherent in the law. However, efforts to address these issues and promote greater equality and inclusion in the democratic process are ongoing.

Representative democracy in the U.S. has come a long way since its inception, but there's still room for improvement. By promoting greater equality, justice, and participation in the democratic process, we can continue strengthening and improving our nation. The U.S. established a representative democracy that prioritizes equality and justice and encourages the active involvement of citizens. The country upholds these ideals by creating a more fair, just, and inclusive society.

Equality, justice, and civic participation are fundamental values in the United States. They are essential to the functioning of a healthy and democratic society. Equality is an absolute value that has shaped the nation's history and has inspired countless Americans to work toward a more just and fair society. Justice ensures that everyone has the same opportunities and protections under the law. Through civic participation in the political process, volunteering in the community, and working to make a difference in the world, people can contribute to the common good and help shape the nation's direction.

Equality, justice, and civic participation are strong values in the United States and are essential to functioning in a healthy and democratic society. By embracing and promoting these values, Americans can help build a better and more just world for themselves and future generations.

REFERENCES

Plato. The Republic. Book 2, pg. 35

Gilens, M., & Page, B. I. "Public opinion has a "near-zero" impact on U.S. law." Studies in Public Opinion, (2014): 45, 1-9. Print.

Connecticut State Advisory Committee memorandum "Voting Rights in U.S. Territories." U.S. Civil Rights Commission Report, October (2021): 1-5. Print.

Alien and Sedition Acts of 1798 (ASA). 1 Stat. 570–573. The National Archives. Web.

Federal Election Campaign Act of 1971 (FECA). Public Law 92-225. The National Archives. Web.

Articles of Confederation and Perpetual Union of 1781 (ACPU). Ch. IX, art. XIII, 1 Stat. 251 The National Archives. Web.

Equal Rights Amendment of 1972 (ERA). S.J. Res. 6, 92d Congress (1972). The National Archives. Web.

Baker v. Carr U.S. Supreme Court (1962). The National Archives. Web.

Kansas-Nebraska Act of 1854 (KNA). Public Law 33-7, 34th Congress, 1st Session. The National Archives. Web.

Reed v. Reed, 404 of 1971 (RvR). U.S. Supreme Court (1971). The National Archives. Web.

Shelby County v. Holder of 2013 (SCvH). SC, U.S. Supreme Court (2013). The National Archives. Web.

Brown v. Board of Education of 1954 (BvB) National Park Service. https://www.nps.gov/articles/brown-v-board-of-education.htm

Federal Election Commission. (n.d.). (FEC). (2022). Home. Retrieved from https://www.fec.gov/

Federal Election Commission (FEC). (2020). Political action committees (PACs). Retrieved from https://www.fec.gov/campaign-activity-and-candidates/political-action-committees-pacs/

Political Parties in the United States (PPUS). (2022). In *Wikipedia.* https://en.wikipedia.org/wiki/Political_Parties_in_the_United_States

U.S. Census Bureau. (2019). American Community Survey (ACS). Retrieved from https://www.census.gov/programs-surveys/acs/

U.S. Census Bureau (USCB). (2020). 2020 Census. Retrieved from https://www.census.gov/programs-surveys/decennial-census.html

U.S. Elections Project (USEP). (2021). Voter Registration and Participation. Retrieved from https://www.electproject.org/voter-registration

U.S. Census Bureau (CPH). (2020). 2020 Census of Population and Housing. Retrieved from https://www.census.gov/data/datasets/time-series/demo/popest/2010s-national-detail.html

United States Department of State(USDS). (n.d.). Home. Retrieved from https://www.state.gov/

"Compromise of 1850" (1850). In *Wikipedia.* https://en.wikipedia.org/wiki/Compromise_of_1850

Wyzant. "25 Highest Rated Citizenship Test Tutors."(2022). Retrieved from https://www.wyzant.com/citizenship_test_tutors.aspx

"The American Anti-Corruption Act: What's In the Act (TAAC)?" (2022). Retrieved from https://anticorruptionact.org/whats-in-the-act/

"Voting rights in the United States." (2022) In *Wikipedia.* https://en.wikipedia.org/wiki/Voting_rights_in_the_United_States

9 798386 837488